Surveillance of Modern Motherhood

Helen Simmons

Surveillance of Modern Motherhood

Experiences of Universal Parenting Courses

Helen Simmons
University of Derby
Derby, UK

ISBN 978-3-030-45362-6   ISBN 978-3-030-45363-3   (eBook)
https://doi.org/10.1007/978-3-030-45363-3

Cover credit: © Alex Linch/shutterstock.com

This Palgrave Macmillan imprint is published by the registered company Springer Nature Switzerland
AG
The registered company address is: Gewerbestrasse 11, 6330 Cham, Switzerland

This book is dedicated to my own mother,
for always encouraging and believing in me, especially when I became a
mother myself.
Thank you for your endless love, humour and support.

The original version of the book was revised: All the abstracts have been corrected. The correction to the book is available at https://doi.org/10.1007/978-3-030-45363-3_9

Acknowledgements

Firstly, I would like to thank the women who offered their personal and emotional insight into the roller coaster experiences of becoming a new mother. I am humbled by and grateful for the trust they gave me.

I would also like to thank my doctoral supervisors Dr. Val Poultney and Dr. Anne Luke whose tremendous support and motivation kept me going from the very beginning of this process and my doctoral examiners Dr. Jane Murray and Dr. Jackie Musgrave for their valuable and extremely constructive feedback.

I would like to thank my colleagues at the University of Derby particularly those within the Early Childhood Studies Team and our Head of Discipline, Sharon Bell. I consider myself to be very lucky to be part of a team that supports each other and that values the diverse work that we do within our sector and discipline.

Huge thanks go to my family and friends that have supported me every step of the way. My husband for his endless patience and for never letting me give up, my children for inspiring me every day and for travelling on this epic journey with me, and my mother-in-law for all of her support. Finally, a massive thanks to my parents for their infinite love and wisdom and for teaching my sisters and I that, with a strong work ethic, we could aspire to be anything we wanted to be in life.

Contents

1 Introduction   1

2 Feminist Post-structuralism as a Worldview   19

3 Emotions, 'Expert' Advice and Support in the Early
   Days of Motherhood   33

4 Surveillance or Support? Political Intervention
   and the Universal Parenting Course   59

5 Feeling Judged: Parenting Culture and Interpersonal
   Surveillance   93

6 The Internalisation of 'Normalising Judgement': The
   'Good Enough' Mother and Silences Within Modern
   Motherhood   119

7 Listening to Mothers: Reflections on Motherhood
   and Support for New Mothers   143

8 Conclusions and Implications for Policy, Research
   and Practice   159

Correction to: Surveillance of Modern Motherhood   C1

Index   173

List of Figures

Fig. 1.1   Government attention on parenting   2
Fig. 1.2   Levels of surveillance within modern motherhood (Based on Henderson et al. 2010)   3
Fig. 2.1   Feminist post-structuralist worldview   30
Fig. 3.1   Key literature within 'historical discourse of expert advice'   39
Fig. 3.2   Key literature within 'online social networking'   42
Fig. 4.1   Key literature within 'Political Intervention'   65
Fig. 4.2   Key literature from 'Evaluations of parenting courses and the "Neuroparenting" discourse'   73
Fig. 5.1   Key literature within 'the rise in parenting culture'   99
Fig. 6.1   Key literature within 'good enough mother' discourse   125
Fig. 7.1   Surveillance of modern motherhood: the conceptual framework   153

List of Tables

Table 3.1   Issues within theme 1   43
Table 3.2   Issues within theme 2   48
Table 4.1   Issues within theme 3   74
Table 4.2   Issues within theme 4   82
Table 5.1   Issues within theme 5   101
Table 6.1   Issues within theme 6   127
Table 7.1   Issues within theme 7   144

1

Introduction

Introduction

The attention on parenting, particularly motherhood, has developed since the Allen (2011, p. xiv) report highlighted the '*right kind of parenting*' and the importance of early intervention within early childhood. With academics in the field of early childhood (Roberts 2010; Murray 2017; Musgrave 2017) recognising and promoting the fundamental importance of valuing children as individuals and as autonomous, researching experts of their own lives though, it seems that this message has not extended to the lives of mothers with policy makers continuously publishing intervention agenda that endorses a standardised formula for parenting. This structural attention is echoed on a wider scale with international examples of parenting intervention programmes explored through the Helping Parent to Parent Report (Clarke et al. 2017) from countries including Sweden, Belgium, USA, Canada, Australia and New Zealand. Findings from the report make links to the success of international programmes in terms of social mobility and their universal approach with the focus on '*equipping parents with a greater understanding of child development*' (Clarke et al. 2017, p. 4). This book will explore the experiences of mothers that have attended a UK based

© The Author(s) 2020
H. Simmons, *Surveillance of Modern Motherhood*,
https://doi.org/10.1007/978-3-030-45363-3_1

1

universal parenting course and deconstruct these experiences through feminist post-structuralist analysis of the dominant discourse within modern motherhood. This book will consider, through multidisciplinary perspectives, including national and international critical literature, research and policy, the experiences of mothers and the support currently available to them.

Information and advice for modern mothers is easily accessible through a variety of platforms, some of which will be explored within this book, including parenting courses, baby manuals, websites, forums and blogs. With this plethora of often conflicting and contradictory 'advice' and representations of motherhood throughout society though, there is a risk that pressures on new mothers are heightened and the opportunity to create anxiety increased. According to Gambles (2010, p. 698), *'parenting is the subject of much contemporary public discussion within the UK as well as other forms of popular culture'*. This attention, according to Furedi (2008, p. 182), ties in with the rise in what can be described as a *'professionalisation of parenting'* whereby parenting is becoming more *'intensive, literally a full time occupation requiring professional support'* (Furedi 2008, p. 15) and is echoed in the increased government focus on parenting as a critical feature for a child's future well-being (Fig. 1.1).

Foucault (1977) related the attention on human behaviour as linking to normalised behaviour that is to be promoted as a *'master narrative'* (Kerrick and Henry 2016, p. 1) through societal structures, surveillance and the use and often misuse of neuroscientific research (Macvarish in Lee et al. 2014; Garrett 2017; Vandenbroeck et al. 2017) and developmental psychology (Burman 2008) by policy makers and those in positions of power.

With Public Health England (2020) stating that *'perinatal mental health problems affect between 10 to 20% of women during pregnancy and*

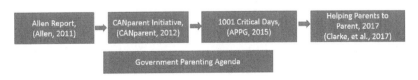

Fig. 1.1   Government attention on parenting

the first year after having a baby' and cost the '*NHS and social services around £1.2 billion annually*' (Public Health England 2020), the need to consider some of the potential factors that can be attributed to adding to these problems is clear. This book will explore the levels of surveillance (Fig. 1.2) that are embedded within modern motherhood and the different experiences and reactions to them, based on the reflections of mothers that have attended Universal Parenting Courses.

A feminist post-structuralist (Davis 1997; Weedon 1997; Baxter 2003) ontological, epistemological and theoretical approach underpinned this research which allowed the experiences of new mothers to be explored and:

> Analyse how they are structured, what power relations they produce and reproduce, where there are resistances and where we might look for weak points more open to challenge and transformation. (Weedon 1997, p. 133)

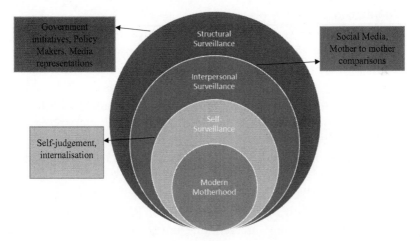

Fig. 1.2 Levels of surveillance within modern motherhood (Based on Henderson et al. 2010)

The Structure of the Book

The book begins with an insight into the research design followed by an exploration of the feminist post-structuralist approach underpinning the research. Following on from this, the book is structured into the key themes that emerged through the analysis. Each theme is presented within a chapter which considers key research and literature associated with that particular theme alongside extracts from the survey and interview responses from the mothers involved in the research. The themes that will be explored in the book are listed below:

– Feminist Post-Structuralism as a worldview:
  Chapter 2 will provide a detailed insight into how feminist and post-structuralist philosophies worked together in this research to drive the exploration and analysis of the dominant discourses and different forms of surveillance embedded within modern motherhood.
– Emotions, 'Expert' Advice and Support in the Early days of Motherhood:
  Chapter 3 will explore historical child-rearing philosophies and trends relating to 'expert' advice including parenting gurus, baby manuals and parenting websites with links to social construction. This chapter will also provide insight into social media as the rising 'expert' and explore the trend in 'blogging' versus social media platforms with an exploration of research relating to the impact on maternal mental health.
– Surveillance or Support? Political Intervention and the Universal Parenting Course:
  Chapter 4 will explore the increased political attention on parenting intervention, following on from the Allen Report (2011). Policies, reports and parenting intervention strategies will be explored and considered.
– Feeling Judged: parenting culture and interpersonal surveillance:
  Chapter 5 will explore research regarding critics of the rise in parenting culture including insight into the perspective that we are currently living in a culture of 'over-parenting', 'parent-scaring' and

'paranoid parenting', exacerbated by the government and media attention on parenting.

– The internalisation of 'normalizing judgement': The 'good enough' mother and silences within modern motherhood:

Chapter 6 centres around Winnicott's (1964) 'good enough' approach and will be considered alongside current research and different perspectives regarding levels of surveillance within modern motherhood.

– Listening to Mothers: Reflections on motherhood and support for new mothers:

Chapter 7 will include insight into the participant views on the support currently offered to new mothers alongside an exploration of the current initiatives and strategies for new mothers.

– Conclusions and implications for policy, research and practice:

Chapter 8 will explore the key findings along with recommendations and reflections for future research, policy and practice.

Research Design and Participants

The first phase of the research was a descriptive survey that included quantitative questions that would provide an insight into the different forms of advice accessed by new mothers. The second phase of the research was semi-structured photo-elicitation interviews that focussed on the wider experiences of modern motherhood and the responses to the different levels of surveillance embedded within those experiences.

Phase 1—Survey

The survey was distributed to mothers of children aged 0–3 years that have attended a universal parenting course. The settings that were approached to complete the survey were from a range of rural and city centre locations including children centres, village halls, churches, community centres and primary schools. The universal parenting courses that were offered within these settings included a range of state sponsored, third sector and private courses. 30 surveys were completed with 7 of these moving into the next phase of the research, after identifying themselves as willing to be interviewed.

Phase 2: Photo-Elicitation Interviews

Given the potentially emotional subject matter, one-to-one open and flexible semi-structured interviews were appropriate within this research and I was particularly drawn to photo-elicitation interviews as a form of semi-structured interviews. Key researchers within the use of visual data within social research, Harper (2002), Banks (2007), and Rose (2012) all emphasise the potential for deep reflection when using photographs within the interview process. It is useful to consider Banks (2007) definition of photo-elicitation as:

> using photographs to evoke comments, memory and discussion in the course of a semi-structured interview.... Can become the basis for a discussion of broader abstractions and generalities: conversely, vague memories can be given sharpness and focus, unleashing a flood of detail. (Banks 2007, p. 65)

Within the context of this research, as Banks (2007) suggests, participants were asked to share existing family photographs, taken since they have been mothers. The aim was to generate reflections of different phases of this new experience, maintaining some level of focus around the factors that lead the participants to attend a parenting course and their wider experiences of early motherhood. The interviews would *'inspire subjects to define how they interpret the events depicted'* (Harper 2002, p. 19) and using the existing family photographs it was hoped, that deeper reflections could be drawn. It was also hoped that the interviews would open opportunities to explore the wider social and cultural issues surrounding why new mothers felt the need to access support, with feminist post-structuralist underpinnings to consider these reflections in terms of the discursive practices embedded within modern motherhood.

There are other opportunities generated through using a photo-elicitation technique, the potential to be an effective 'ice-breaker' is one not to be ignored. By passing the control of who selects the photographs to the participant, the aim is that power divides and that any differences in status are also reduced. Interviews taking place within participant's own homes, discussing their own photographs and using them to generate informal and flexible discussions would all go some way to alleviating potential anxieties and awkwardness. Banks (2007) claims that '*direct eye contact need not be maintained, but instead interviewee and interviewer can both turn to the photograph as a kind of neutral third party*' (Banks 2007, p. 65).

The potential for photographs to empower participants and help to generate deeper more meaningful reflections was something desirable, but it was important to acknowledge the potential '*emotional and intense*' (Rose 2012, p. 305) nature that the interview may take as a result of the inclusion of photographs. Asking people to relive and draw upon experiences of new motherhood could be a joyful and deeply gratifying experience, but there was also the potential, depending on the experience of the mother, for other feelings to emerge. Whilst it was the deepest, richest and sincerest reflections from experiences that would benefit the research, it must not be at the emotional expense of participants and this was considered sensitively during the research design process. Further detail regarding the participants and the interviews can be found below. Please note, in order to protect the anonymity of the participants, identification numbers are used for participants from the survey phase of the research and pseudonyms for participants in the interview phase:

The Interview Participants

Claire: This interview took place in March 2016 in Claire's home. Claire had attended a universal parenting course at her local Children's Centre near where she lives in a town and civil parish within the East Midlands. She had 2 young children (aged 2 and 1 years old at the time of the interview) and both children were present during the interview. Claire was 38 years of age at the time of the interview.

Jenny: This interview took place in April 2016 in Jenny's home. Jenny had attended a universal parenting course through an NCT location near where she lives in a town within the East Midlands. She had 1 young child (aged 13 months at the time of the interview) and her child was present during the interview. Jenny was 33 years of age at the time of the interview.

Priya: This interview took place in April 2016 in Priya's home. Priya had attended a universal parenting course at her local Children's Centre near where she lives in a large village within the East Midlands. She had 2 young children (aged 6 and 3 years old at the time of the interview), neither children were present during the interview. Priya was 35 years of age at the time of the interview.

Ruth: This interview took place in April 2016 in Ruth's home. Ruth had attended a universal parenting course at her local Children's Centre near where she lives in a large village within South Yorkshire. She had 2 young children (aged 5 years old and 4 months at the time of the interview) and her youngest child was present during the interview. Ruth was 35 years of age at the time of the interview.

Gemma: This interview took place in May 2016 in Gemma's home. Gemma had attended a universal parenting course at her local village hall near where she lives in a large village in the East Midlands. She had 2 young children (aged 3 and 4 months at the time of the interview) and her youngest child was present during the interview, although asleep in a different room. Gemma was 32 years of age at the time of the interview.

Louise: This interview took place in May 2016 at a restaurant near Louise's place of work in South Yorkshire. Louise had attended a universal parenting course at her local Children's Centre near where she lives in a suburb of South Yorkshire. She had 2 young children (aged 5 and 2 years old at the time of the interview), neither children were present during the interview. Louise was 35 years of age at the time of the interview.

Kate: This interview took place in June 2016 at a restaurant near Kate's place of work in the East Midlands. Kate had attended a universal parenting course at her local Children's Centre near where she lives in a suburb of South Yorkshire. She had 2 young children (aged 4 and 1 years old at the time of the interview) neither children were present during the interview. Kate was 35 years of age at the time of the interview.

An Ethical Approach

Reflexivity and self-awareness were essential aspects of ensuring an ethical approach to this research and my position within it. Through a deep exploration of the experiences that influenced my own ontological position it was possible to develop a meaningful approach to exploring and analysing the experiences of the mothers I would be working with. The work of Ackerly and True (2008, p. 693) provided a useful platform in which to consider my own '*reflexivity in practice*'. As highlighted throughout this book, my research position was closely aligned to a post-structuralist perspective from the outset. My own awareness of government agenda, initiatives and parenting 'experts' may have influenced the position that I would gravitate towards and this was developed further through the academic discipline that I am part of which aims to critique and question the regulatory structures that govern our society. Through an '*attentiveness to epistemology*' (Ackerly and True 2008, p. 695) though, I began to see my ontological position shift with the development of the literature and through deeper reflections from my own experiences as a mother and of observing other mothers. This shift developed into a recognition that a purely post-structuralist approach could serve to discount the incidents where mothers would demonstrate resistance and agency in their individual experiences. Through acknowledging my underlying suspicions that a post-structuralist perspective alone would not be sufficient within this research; I was able to see that the:

> purpose is not to privilege the epistemological standpoint of the most marginalized but rather to adopt an epistemological perspective that requires the scholar to inform her inquiry with a range of perspectives. (Ackerly and True 2008, p. 696)

Acknowledging subjectivity within the experiences of mothers is a fundamental part of the ethics within this research. Post-structuralist theory, as stated by Weedon (1997, p. 21) '*theorizes subjectivity as a site of disunity and conflict, central to the processes of political change and to preserving the status quo*'. Whilst this may have proved evident through the experiences of participants, within my ontological perspective and in order to retain my ethical position, I felt that I had to acknowledge the potential for autonomy within the experiences of mothers including the possibility that not all mothers would react to the dominant discourses in the same way.

Critical self-reflection at each stage was essential in order to maintain this attention to my ontological approach and for me, this involved maintaining a reflexive diary. This helped me to not only express thoughts, feelings and ideas but also to understand the '*key influences acting upon the development of the research*' (Oliver 2010, p. 116). Through the process of being '*reflexively self-aware*' (Forbes 2008, p. 453) I was able to consider the different identities that I held within this research and how they and my ontological position along with it, would change and '*shift positions*' (Forbes 2008, p. 453) over time and experience. An example of this occurred when I attended a conference on the same day that I interviewed my first participant. The conference was centred around parenting culture and was extremely critical of parenting courses and any such intervention as undermining to parents. At this point my own ontological perspective was such that I could see the potential harm that formulaic and homogenous support for new mothers could have. I was therefore surprised by my reaction and the unshakable feeling I had that the underlying suggestion that all mothers, without exception, were docile victims of modern parenting culture did mothers a fundamental disservice. It was reflections such as this along with a recognition that the voices and real-life experiences of mothers were missing through this narrative that resulted in the shifting ontological perspective towards a feminist post-structuralist worldview. As stated by Ackerly and True (2008, p. 702), it is through this attention to epistemology and deep reflections on the position of the researcher that it is possible for the research question to be formed '*out of engagement with the real world experiences of non-elites*'. Incidents such as this, along with engagement with literature and policy relating to attention on parenting, particularly motherhood, influenced the underpinning aim within this research which was to hear from the mothers themselves about their experiences of attending a parenting course and their own reflections about modern motherhood.

Women Interviewing Women, Ethics and Trustworthiness

Whilst I acknowledge that I am a researcher and an academic, I am also a woman and a mother and I hoped that participants would find it possible to open up to me in a way that would help to break down any potential power barriers. However, it is important not to be naive here: I was still an investigator with an overall aim and that could not be ignored. Letherby (2003, p. 113) points out that:

> although a researcher may feel sympathy or empathy with respondents, her involvement with them affects her working life, her career. Similarly, respondents may consciously be using the research and the researcher as a receptacle for their emotions.

Through reflexivity, *'attentiveness to relationships'* (Ackerly and True 2008, p. 703), an awareness of the way I presented myself and by taking a flexible and informal approach to the interviews, I aimed to build a non-hierarchical and friendly atmosphere, which is a vital part of the researcher–participant relationship. This breakdown in barriers with participants would relax them and encourage reflection, and I accepted that this may require some level of self-disclosure particularly in relation, to some degree, to my own experiences of motherhood. In terms of the impact on the quality of the data though, I was aware that this open approach would have implications in the way I would interpret the responses. It was therefore important for me to recognise the subjectivity of the participants. Their experiences of motherhood may not have been the same as mine as on the basis of *'race, class, age and cultural background'* (Weedon 1997, p. 91) and the feminist post-structuralist approach supported this subjective lens.

Relating back to my position as an insider–outsider researcher required some acknowledgement that my identity would shift (Ackerly and True 2008) during the course of the research process. Whilst I have a *'shared identity'* (Alasuutari et al. 2008, p. 333) with respondents as a mother; I am also an outsider with, what could potentially be perceived as, an aim to use personal experiences for my own gain. As explored, this shifting identity required a deep level of reflexivity, attention to shifting power relations (Ackerly and True 2008) and sensitivity on my part from the beginning and it was useful to consider the work of Oakley (2005) who reflected on her experiences of interviewing women. Her reflections are particularly relatable to this research as she explored factors that must be considered in relation to women interviewing women and how this relationship can often become '*something which existed beyond the limits of question asking and answering*' (Oakley 2005, p. 224).

This is particularly true when, as highlighted above, the aim within the early stages of the interview was to relax participants and develop some level of rapport through the shared identity and '*natural empathy*' (Cohen et al. 2018, p. 236) of being mothers of young children. Oakley (2005) goes further in her reflections and explores the interview process from a feminist perspective and how this position led her to the decision to move away from a '*textbook code of ethics*' (Oakley 2005, p. 225). Rather than claiming to take an entirely objective position within the interview, the development of a relationship, building up of trust and rapport means that the interview may easily take a turn from clear cut, 'clean' questions into a more conversational, two-way communication. From a feminist position, Oakley suggests that a deviation from '*taken-for-granted sociological assumptions about the role of the interviewer*' (Oakley 2005, p. 226) in favour of an approach that will encourage deeper, sincerer reflections from women about their lives and experiences. The role of the interviewer then is to provide a more relational environment whereby rather than just extracting information, experiences could be shared in a non-judgemental, non-hierarchical way making possible '*the articulated and recorded commentary of women on the very personal business of being a female in a patriarchal capitalist society*' (Oakley 2005, p. 226).

The consideration of the methods that have been explored in this section moved this research towards an original design. However, in order to produce trustworthiness (Gray 2014; Nowell et al. 2017) there were other factors to consider. Whilst my position as an insider–outsider researcher and feminist post-structuralist worldview meant that my own previous experience as a practitioner and mother would impact on the research, it was important to maintain an open mind throughout the research process and this involved reflexivity throughout the planning, designing and analysis of the research. As identified by Creswell (2009) qualitative research can be categorised as interpretive research. This approach not only raises ethical concerns but also personal ones from the perspective of the researcher:

> With these concerns in mind, inquirers explicitly identify reflexively their biases, values and personal background, such as gender, history, culture, and socio-economic status that may shape their interpretations formed during the study. (Creswell 2009, p. 177)

That is not to say that all objectivity can be entirely removed. As explored, my own personal experiences could both enhance and hinder the interpretations of the research findings. Indeed, holding true to the feminist post-structuralist worldview required a more reflexive approach to the research than simply expecting my lived experiences as a woman to be enough. As Hammington (2009) states '*a feminist standpoint requires an effort at standing back to gain a holistic picture of power struggles*' (Hammington 2009, p. 54). At the same time though, linking back to the work of Oakley, a successful interview, from a feminist perspective will take a '*no intimacy without reciprocity*' (Oakley 2005, p. 226) stance, and whilst recognising the need to proceed with caution in terms of any potential bias, in agreement with the work of Oakley, I did not '*regard it as reasonable to adopt a purely exploitative attitude to interviewees as a source of data*' (Oakley 2005, p. 225). This is particularly true given the sensitive and personal nature of the subject matter.

Similarly, Mauthner et al. (2002) recognise how valuable the development of rapport can be within the interview process but how careful consideration of results needs to take place. When, what they call '*over easy rapport*' takes place for example '*when interviewees said: 'You know what I mean', she tended to reply: 'I know', partly deliberately to build rapport but also intuitively because she felt she genuinely did know*' (Mauthner et al. 2002, p. 117). It was important to consider this before the interviews took place, the importance of rapport should not replace the trustworthiness of the conversations taking place and the interpretations and analysis of them, and this highlights the dangers of '*reading between the lines*' (Mauthner et al. 2002, p. 117) within interpretations of interviews. The ethics of women interviewing women and the consideration of trustworthiness formed an important part of this investigation, there are now other ethical considerations that needed to be explored in relation to research as a whole.

Protection of the Participants

The feminist post-structuralist worldview that underpins this research is one that ensured attention to the '*privilege of being able to do the research and to the power relationships that are part of the research process*' (Ackerly and True 2008, p. 701). An example of this came from the decision not to ask participants to identify themselves within a particular class structure as this would not be in keeping with the philosophical worldview and may imply from the outset, an unhelpful feeling of being judged.

The attention to the protection of participants also included a consideration to the potential psychological risk regarding the disclosure of potentially emotional responses from participates. It was outlined, through the ethical approval stage that should it be deemed necessary, which fortunately it was not, participants would be directed to their health visitor or doctor for appropriate support. Similarly, it was possible that during the interviews, participants would disclose information or ask for my advice, I would be clear that I was conducting the interviews in the capacity of a researcher and not as a health professional. Should participants require further assistance or advice on a particular topic, they would be sensitively directed to the relevant and appropriate support. Care was taken throughout the process to '*desist immediately from any actions, ensuing from the research process that can cause emotional or other harm*' (BERA 2011, p. 10).

As stated in the BERA (2011, p. 10) ethical guidelines '*researchers must recognise that participants may experience distress or discomfort in the research process and must take all necessary steps to reduce the sense of intrusion and to put them at ease'*. Similarly, within the feminist post-structuralist lens of this research and in order to retain integrity as a researcher, I was mindful throughout the research of my responsibility to, as outlined by Cohen et al. (2018, p. 133), ensure that participants do not *'leave the research situation with greater anxiety or lower levels of self-esteem than they came with'*. A reflexive journal was kept throughout the research process in order to reflect on each interview and recognise my own role within the research. This included acknowledging when participant reflections regarding sensitive aspects of motherhood chimed with my own experiences and I found that keeping a diary helped me to be reflexive throughout the process.

Summary

This book explores the reflections and experiences of mothers of children aged 0–3 years that have attended universal parenting courses. The aim of the research was to gain a deeper understanding of the factors that motivated mothers to attend a universal parenting course and to explore the wider experiences of early modern motherhood in the UK.

In order to develop this understanding, the research explored participant perceptions of any benefit or otherwise in attending a parenting course and also considered the different forms of parenting advice accessed by mothers and how this provides an insight into the wider constructs and experiences of modern motherhood.

Ultimately, the goal of this research was to consider the social and cultural pressures within modern motherhood in relation to different levels of surveillance (Henderson et al. 2010) and to produce new knowledge for practice within the early years and health sectors in relation to the support currently offered to new mothers. This began with an exploration of the dominant discourses within the literature and research surrounding early experiences of motherhood.

References

Ackerly, B., & True, J. (2008). Reflexivity in Practice: Power and Ethics in Feminist Research on International Relations. *The International Studies Association, 10*(8), 693–707.

Alasuutari, P., Bickman, L., & Brannen, J. (2008). *The Sage Handbook of Social Research Methods*. London: Sage.

Allen, G. (2011). *Early Intervention: The Next Steps, an Independent Report to Her Majesty's Government by Graham Allen MP*. London: The Stationary Office.

All Party Parliamentary Group (APPG). (2015). *Conception to Age 2: First 1001 Days. Perinatal Inquiry—Evidence Sessions on First 1001 Days*. UK.

Banks, M. (2007). *Using Visual Data in Qualitative Research*. London: Sage.

Baxter, J. (2003). *Positioning Gender in Discourse: A Feminist Methodology*. Hampshire: Palgrave Macmillan.

British Educational Research Association (BERA). (2011). *Ethical Guidelines for Educational Research*. London: Council of the British Educational Research Association.

Burman, E. (2008). *Deconstructing Developmental Psychology* (2nd ed.). London: Routledge.

CANparent. (2012). *CANparent—Classes and Advice Network*. Available at http://www.parentinguk.org/canparent/network. Accessed 13 January 2020.

Clarke, B., Younas, F., Project Team and Family Kids and Youth. (2017). *Helping Parents to Parent*. London: Social Mobility Commission.

Cohen, L., Manion, L., & Morrison, K. (2018). *Research Methods in Education* (8th ed.). London: Routledge.

Creswell, J. W. (2009). *Research Design: Qualitative, Quantitative and Mixed Methods Approaches* (3rd ed.). London: Sage.

Davis, B. (1997). The Subject of Post-structuralism: A Reply to Alison Jones. *Gender and Education, 9*(3), 271–283.

Forbes, J. (2008). Reflexivity in Professional Doctorate Research. *Reflective Practice: International and Multidisciplinary Perspectives, 9*(4), 449–460.

Foucault, M. (1977). *Discipline and Punish: The Birth of the Prison*. London: Penguin.

Furedi, F. (2008). *Paranoid Parenting: Why Ignoring the Experts May be Best for Your Child*. Wiltshire: Continuum.

Gambles, R. (2010). Supernanny, Parenting and a Pedagogical State. *Citizenship Studies, 14*(6), 697–709.

Garrett, P. M. (2017). Wired: Early Intervention and the 'Neuromolecular Gaze'. *British Journal of Social Work, 48*(3), 656–674.

Gray, D. E. (2014). *Doing Research in the Real World*. London: Sage.

Hammington, M. (2009). *The Social Policy of Jane Addams*. Urbana and Chicago, USA: The University of Illinois press.

Harper, D. (2002). Talking About Pictures: A Case for Photo Elicitation. *Visual Studies, 17*(1), 13–26.

Henderson, A., Harmon, S., & Houser, J. (2010). A New State of Surveillance: Applying Michael Foucault to Modern Motherhood. *Surveillance and Society, 7*(3/4), 231–247.

Kerrick, M., & Henry, R. L. (2016). 'Totally in Love': Evidence of a Master Narrative for How New Mothers Should Feel About Their Babies. *Sex Roles, 76*(1), 1–16.

Lee, E., Bristow, J., Faircloth, C., & Macvarish, J. (2014). *Parenting Culture Studies*. London: Palgrave Macmillan.

Letherby, G. (2003). *Feminist Research in Theory and Practice*. Buckingham: Open University Press.

Mauthner, M., Birch, M., Jessop, J., & Miller, T. (2002). *Ethics in Qualitative Research*. London: Sage.

Murray, J. (2017). *Building Knowledge in Early Childhood Education: Young Children Are Researchers'*. London: Routledge.

Musgrave, J. (2017). *Supporting Children's Health and Wellbeing*. London: Sage.

Nowell, L. S., Norris, J. M., & White, D. E. (2017). Thematic Analysis: Striving to Meet the Trustworthiness Criteria. *International Journal of Qualitative Methods, 16*, 1–13.

Oakley, A. (2005). *The Ann Oakley Reader*. Bristol: Policy Press.

Oliver, P. (2010). *Understanding the Research Process*. London: Sage Study.

Public Health England. (2020). *Perinatal Mental Health*. Available at https://www.gov.uk/government/publications/better-mental-health-jsna-toolkit/4-perinatal-mental-health. Accessed 13 January 2020.

Roberts, R. (2010). *Wellbeing from Birth*. London: Sage.

Rose, G. (2012). *Visual Methodologies: An Introduction to Researching with Visual Materials*. London: Sage.

Vandenbroeck, M., De Vos, J., Fias, W., Mariett Olsson, L., Penn, H., Wastell, D., & White, S. (2017). *Constructions of Neuroscience in Early Childhood Education*. London: Routledge.

Weedon, C. (1997). *Feminist Practice and Poststructuralist Theory* (2nd ed.). Oxford: Blackwell.

Winnicott, D. (1964). *The Child, the Family and the Outside World*. London: Penguin Books.

2

Feminist Post-structuralism as a Worldview

Introduction

As identified within Chapter 1, feminist post-structuralism is the underpinning worldview within which this research was framed. It is important therefore to begin this chapter with a detailed insight into how these philosophies worked together to drive the analysis of the literature regarding the dominant discourses within modern motherhood.

Feminist Post-structuralist Worldview

This section will begin with an insight into the post-structuralist concepts. The discussion will then move on to justify, in greater detail, why the conceptual framework could not be aligned, in its entirety, to post-structuralism alone and how, through a combined feminist post-structuralist worldview, the opportunities to explore the experiences of the participants from a range of possible perspectives were heightened.

© The Author(s) 2020
H. Simmons, *Surveillance of Modern Motherhood*,
https://doi.org/10.1007/978-3-030-45363-3_2

Post-structuralism

Post-structuralist theory challenges the structures that result in members of society behaving in a certain way. Drawing from Foucault's (1977) exploration of 'Panoptism' and his disciplinary technologies, it is possible to explore modern motherhood through a post-structuralist lens and consider how current motherhood ideologies have become the norm that all mothers must strive towards. This, according to post-structuralism does not just refer to the surveillance and discipline from others, but the internalisation and self-surveillance of individuals to achieve the norm and behave in the 'right way'. This way the behaviour of others, in this case, mothers is 'naturalised' and the desired, normalised behaviour is fostered. It is through the process of Foucault's disciplinary technologies; surveillance, judgement and correct training that power is asserted. Dreyfus and Rabinow (1982, p. 157) explain the subtlety of this movement on members of society; '*it does this not by crushing them or lecturing them, but by "humble" procedures of training and distribution*'. That is not to say that a solution is offered through the lens of post-structuralism. The aim of such research is not to rectify a 'problem', but to provide an understanding of the origins of a particular issue and to explore the meaning and reflect upon the discourses and power relations that may have led to the behaviours within motherhood that we now consider to be the norm. This will begin with an identification of what Foucault labels the 'dominant discourses' (Foucault 1977).

Dominant discourse within society are practices or behaviours that over time, appear to be given 'the stamp of truth'. These practices become '*highly ritualized*' (Foucault 1977, p. 184) according to Foucault and combined with the '*deployment of force*' (Foucault 1977, p. 184), they serve to form '*the establishment of truth*' (Foucault 1977, p. 184). The acceptance of these dominant discourses over time and changes in both social policy and practice within services offered as support to families, strengthen further the expected and normalised behaviour by members of society.

The notion of the 'expert' (Davis 2012) as socially constructed, for example, can be associated with Foucauldian concepts of truth when exploring both historical and contemporary forms of correct training.

Foucault (1977) considers the *'simple instruments'* (Rabinow 1991, p. 188) used within society to train acceptable and correct unacceptable behaviour. Such instruments, as explored by Foucault can be compared to the philosophy and outline of current parenting education. Identified by Foucault as *'hierarchical observation'*, *'normalizing judgement'* and *'their combination in a procedure that is specific to it – the examination'* (Rabinow 1991, p. 188). Each of Foucault's instruments can be explored and compared to current parenting education programmes.

The first instrument to explore is *'hierarchical observation'* (Foucault 1977, p. 170) and is associated with *'hierarchized, continuous and functional surveillance'* (Foucault 1977, p. 176), the concept that through a top-down approach, the behaviour of others will be constantly observed by those in positions of power, whether that be in the form of an educational environment or in this case, within parenting practice. Correlating to the work of Lee et al. (2014) who, whilst making no direct reference to Foucault in their work, question the philosophy that underpins parenting education programmes and the idea that good parenting is something that can be learnt by those willing to engage in a parenting programme, Foucault also comments on forms of correct training as originating from a place of power and judgement. Both Foucault (1977) and more recently, Lee et al. (2014) suggest that the idea that those in a hierarchical position in which they can observe the behaviour of others and pass judgement accordingly is something worth exploring and questioning.

The second of Foucault's instruments within correct training is *'normalizing judgement'* (Foucault 1977, p. 177). This is, arguably at the very heart of the aim of parenting education. Through the initial practice of hierarchical observation and structural surveillance, judgement is passed, and a system of correct training formed. The government focus on parenting as a *'public health issue'* (Clarke et al. 2017, p. 4) and on normalizing parenting courses to become as routine as antenatal classes can be connected to the ideas of Foucault that the *'power of normalization imposes homogeneity'* (Foucault 1977, p. 184). In the form of parenting education in the UK, this would refer to a standardised programme of child rearing and parenting. Within parenting education, normalising judgement may go some way to explaining why some mothers struggle to feel 'good enough' (Winnicott 1964; Currie 2008) as they compare themselves to others and feel judged as a result of constant hierarchical observation and surveillance. The overall impact, therefore, relating not only to parenting education, but to parenting practice overall.

Henderson et al. (2010) in their investigation of modern motherhood apply Foucauldian concepts of surveillance to what they found to be the most powerful level of surveillance; '*interpersonal (mother to mother), not structural (media to mothers) level*' (Henderson et al. 2010, p. 232). The work of Henderson et al. (2010) gives a new lens within which to explore the experience of modern mothers and they also point out the increased pressure mothers place on themselves in terms of 'self-surveillance' whereby, unconsciously they compare themselves to other mothers and judge themselves harshly in terms of parenting ability. Within their research they found that '*not only are mothers blaming themselves and feeling guilty about the job they do as parents, but it is their self-blame and guilt that leads to a higher level of pressure to be perfect*' (Henderson et al. 2010, p. 240). The different forms of surveillance suggested by Henderson et al.'s (2010) investigation provide an interesting way of viewing the pressures felt by mothers to be 'good enough'. It is important to consider the way these forms of surveillance, whether through the media or state surveillance, surveillance from other mothers or self-surveillance, add to the pressures felt by mothers and link to the motivating factors in attending a parenting course.

This struggle to meet societal expectations, from a post-structuralist perspective, can also be connected to the final of Foucault's instruments for correct training; '*the examination*' (Foucault 1977, p. 184). It is at this point, according to Foucault that the hierarchical observation and normalising judgements are combined. A result is formed here, a '*normalizing gaze, a surveillance that makes it possible to qualify, to classify and to punish*' (Foucault 1977, p. 184). At this moment, within parenting education, a mother may begin to feel some of that control return, to feel 'good enough' (Winnicott 1964; Currie 2008) as a mother. Foucault refers to the examination as the point which '*establishes over individuals a visibility through which one differentiates them and judges them*' (Foucault 1977, p. 184). Self-judgement occurs here too, the comparison of one's self to another within the process of correct training leading to an internalisation of the expected societal behaviours. Considering self-judgement in light of Foucault's concepts of surveillance, discipline and punishment is useful. The instruments of correct training form rules and regulations which can be applied to the correct way of parenting.

Foucault further explored the effects of continuous surveillance through his application of Bentham's '*Panopticon*' and his discussion of a system which increases the psychological control over inmates who '*must never know whether he is being looked at any one moment, but he must be sure that he may always be so*' (Foucault 1977, p. 201). This method of discipline creates order based on the constant surveillance and '*permanent visibility that assures the automatic functioning of power*' (Foucault 1977, p. 201). In the context of parenting education, the instruments of correct training, together with the surveillance of society through a continuous '*faceless gaze*' (Foucault 1977, p. 215) heightens the expectations and pressures of modern motherhood. This perspective could therefore, provide insight into the way in which '*women's subjectivities are structured, in part, through the mastery of technique and specialized knowledge required to move, adorn and otherwise manage a feminine body*' (McCann and Kim 2017, p. 363).

Foucault's exploration of '*panopticism*' can also be considered in relation to motherhood from the perspective of the normalising judgements that dictates an appropriate way to behave as a mother and also on a wider level, the surveillance through interaction with other mothers, and the internalised pressure mothers place on themselves. Using post-structuralist concepts this relates to the internalisation of the panoptic machine, the way the application of societal norms, through the process of surveillance of mothers, '*add to their internal and specific function a role of external surveillance, developing around themselves a whole margin of lateral controls*' (Foucault 1977, p. 211). The stigma and fear of punishment, in this case being potentially labelled as a 'bad mother' or 'not coping', according to this perspective would lead mothers to act in accordance with the rules.

Foucault's ideas can also be considered through the work of Rose (1999, p. 1) who explores the attention of the family, particularly from a psychological perspective as developing a means by those in positions of power to '*govern the soul*'. Rose's work, whilst not aiming to critique psychology as a body of knowledge, does seek to explore the way that such discourses have '*rendered knowable the normal and pathological functioning of humans*' and how this knowledge has subsequently been transformed into '*problems offered by political, economic, and moral strategies*' (Rose 1999, p. xxvii). Rose's work offers a useful insight into the focus on parenting education, particularly when considered alongside the parenting intervention programmes that use psychoanalytical and neurodevelopmental research to underpin their strategies.

The post-structuralist emphasis on members of society and how their exposure to '*the establishment of truth*' (Foucault 1977, p. 184) leads to normalised behaviour are refuted by some though. Indeed, it is recognised by feminist writers (McNay 1992; Ramazanoglu 1993) that there are tensions between feminist and post-structuralist thought that cannot be ignored, many feminist arguments centre on the limitations of post-structuralist writing to explain female autonomy:

> This lack of rounded theory of subjectivity or agency conflicts with a fundamental aim of the feminist project: to rediscover and re-evaluate the experiences of women. (McNay 1992, p. 3)

Given the tensions between the feminist and post-structuralist worldviews, it is important to now consider how they may work alongside each other and in fact, complement each other and bring multiple possibilities and reactions to the experiences of modern mothers.

Feminist Post-structuralism

Whilst it could be suggested that the '*emancipatory stance of feminism and the deconstructive purpose of post-structuralism should be seen as dichotomous*' (Baxter 2003, p. 14), the development of a feminist post-structuralist approach makes it possible to consider the construction of normalised judgements and the internalisation of these structures whilst also acknowledging the possibility and opportunity for agency and resistance within the experiences of mothers.

One of the major enterprises of feminist post-structuralist theory has been
the deconstruction of female subjectivity and the analysis of the extent to
which women's experiences of themselves as subjects may be constructed
within discourses, practices and power relationships. (Baxter 2003, p. 33)

Similar to the post-structuralist perspectives outlined above, feminist
research, through its exploration of the contested ideologies of motherhood (Douglas and Michaels 2005; Beaupre Gillespie and Schwartz
Temple 2011) and the cultural contradiction (Hays 1996) within them
have attempted to offer insight into the constructs of motherhood
within modern society. Explored further within the wider dominant
discourses, feminist theories of motherhood ideologies (Douglas and
Michaels 2005; Beaupre Gillespie and Schwartz Temple 2011) aim to
expose the discursive practices and messages portrayed within modern
culture that motherhood should be considered something natural and
instinctive and how these messages serve to contradict and confuse
mothers who are encouraged simultaneously to attend parenting courses
in order to learn the 'right way' to mother.

A combined feminist post-structuralist lens provides an opportunity
'which reveals what is going on in women's lives' (Letherby 2003, p. 6).
Maintaining a feminist post-structuralist epistemological and ontological
position throughout this research allowed the constructions of human
behaviour in this case, motherhood, to be explored whilst also providing
the opportunity for multiple possibilities in the form of agency and
autonomy to be considered.

This research, as within the ethos of feminist research, maintained
respectful considerations of participants and acknowledges opportunities for the resistance of the dominant discourses, as reported by Miller
(2005):

The topic of mothering and motherhood is an area of social research that
has greatly benefited from a range of feminist contributions, not least
identifying it as an area worth scrutiny. (Miller 2005, p. 7)

Drawing on the work of Foucault, Baxter (2003, p. 37) proposes
that 'post-structuralist inquiry may indeed support feminist projects with

an intent to liberate subjugated groups as long as these aim to promote the free play of multiple voices within diverse contexts'. Within her research and the development of a feminist post-structural discourse analysis theory, Baxter suggests that using these two approaches together produces a *'productive contradiction'* (Baxter 2003, p. 2) whereby criticisms surrounding the post-structuralist lack of recognition of agency and resistance of the dominant discourses embedded into motherhood practice, can be explored more deeply within a feminist lens. Similarly, criticism of emancipatory feminism politics including the *'quest to expose the gendered nature of society or the structural inequalities it produces'* (Ahall 2012, p. 106) can be explored within a post-structuralist lens, a modern perspective can be formed which reviews some of the *'old assumptions'* and new constructions of motherhood can be considered.

This also echoes the work of Henderson et al. (2010) and their levels of surveillance, whereby rather than exploring motherhood from an oppressive male-dominated feminist perspective, it becomes possible to consider how interpersonal surveillance between mothers impact on the early experiences of motherhood, and adds to the internalisation of the normalising judgements and constructs of feeling 'good enough' (Winnicott 1964; Currie 2008).

With Baxter's (2003, p. 2) notion of the *'productive contradiction'* in mind, it is also possible, within a feminist post-structuralist perspective, to recognise that *'women are not passive recipients of these constructions'* (Johnson et al. 2009, p. 901). Whilst this research is interested in the wider social issues rather than exploring the individual experiences alone, it is still possible to consider experiences of motherhood in relation to the discursive practices, *'master narratives'* (Kerrick and Henry 2016, p. 1) or *'storylines'* (Davis 1997, p. 275) that are associated with motherhood on a wider level. Similarly, Baxter (2003, p. 12) suggests that *'the local meaning of talk always work within, represent and reconstitute broader discursive structures, relations and processes'*.

As previously highlighted, the lack of recognition around the notion of self-regulation or autonomy is one of the major criticisms of post-structuralism as a philosophy (Ramazanoglu 1993; McNay 1992). Criticism include the assumption that women are *'docile bodies'* (Foucault 1977, p. 136) that show little or no ability to resist the dominant discourses they are subjected to or at the very least, negotiate these constructs to suit their own identity and parenting practice (Johnson et al. 2009). This assumption, arguably, does members of society a disservice and goes no way to explaining why and how some of these members contest the normalising judgements and challenge the cultural practices that are embedded within society as the norm.

With this in mind, an advocate of feminist post-structuralist theory; Weedon (1997) accepts the criticisms of post-structuralism and the perception that the experiences of others are socially constructed through the dominant discourses and therefore '*deny the authenticity of individual experience*' (Weedon 1997, p. 121), she goes on to suggest though, that '*what Foucault's work offers feminists, however, is, a contextualisation of experiences and an analysis of its constitution and ideological power*' (Weedon 1997, p. 121). By bringing both feminism and post-structuralism together it is possible to provide the opportunity for women to reflect on their experiences, constructs of motherhood and '*choose from the options available*' (Weedon 1997, p. 121). In this sense, feminism and post-structuralism will work together to produce a deeper insight into motherhood through reflection on, and possible challenging of, the dominant discourses.

Similarly, returning to the advancement of Foucault's work through Rose (1999, p. vii), subjectivity is explored through history in relation to how events and changes over time have '*gone to make up our current ways of understanding and relating to ourselves as human beings with a certain subjectivity*'. In these terms, Rose is interested in how psychological theory itself '*celebrates values of autonomy and self-realization*' but how, when used by those involved in 'structural surveillance' (Henderson et al. 2010) to explain human behaviour can serve to '*fabricate subjects – human men, women and children – capable of bearing the burdens of liberty*' (Rose 1999, p. viii).

Through his exploration and discussion of disciplinary and normalising technologies, Foucault was interested in the '*bio-power*' (Dreyfus and Rabinow 1982, p. 133) associated with the internalisation of different social and cultural norms within society. Feminist writers acknowledge Foucault's '*important contribution to social theory*' (McNay 1992, p. 9). Similarly, Ramazanoglu (1993, p. 5) suggests that '*Foucault's work provides a sharp critique of some of the ways in which feminists have set about explaining gendered power'*. Whilst contributors to Ramazanoglu's (1993) edited volume express their concerns about some of Foucault's assumptions and the limitations towards feminist theory, they also acknowledge *'what he has usefully done is to provide new means for thinking through some of the areas of understanding social life which have proven contradictory and problematic'* (Ramazanoglu 1993, p. 5). Again, in support of how feminism and post-structuralism can work together is Baxter:

> What a specifically post-structuralist approach offers feminism, with its emphasis upon specific and localised forms of transformative action, is a politically confidence approach to all forms of research inquiry. (Baxter 2003, p. 41)

In consideration of how a post-structuralist lens could work alongside a feminist lens, particularly in relation to this research, I believed it was possible for the two philosophies to work alongside one another. Both philosophies aim to explore how the dominant discourses create power relations that determine the lived experiences of others and how systems and structures can be considered and reflected upon, in order to reveal the normalisation and internalisation of a particular regime. Together, a combined feminist post-structuralist epistemological approach allows for a broader interpretation and exploration of the experiences of modern motherhood. With the focus on exploring the early experiences of modern motherhood, specifically through the eyes of those who have chosen to engage with parenting courses, a feminist post-structuralist lens acts as a way of *'aligning subjectivity with cultural ideologies of motherhood'* (Johnson et al. 2009, p. 900).

Another key supporter of the feminist post-structuralist approach is Davis (1997) who suggests that this approach, rather than ignoring the importance of individual experience, seeks to *'enable us to see the subject's fictionality, whilst recognising how powerful fictions are in constituting what we take to be real'* (Davis 1997, p. 272). In this respect, the idea of the storylines, *'fictionality'* or *'master narrative'* (Kerrick and Henry 2016, p. 1) by which we live are the important constructs that must be explored and understood more deeply and a feminist post-structuralist approach provides a lens for the exploration of the opportunities for both the oppression and empowerment of women within modern motherhood. According to Davis (1997), a feminist post-structuralist perspective embraces the contradiction and opportunities within these combined approaches, to bring about change. Davis suggests that:

> Linear forms of logic are too constraining for those of us who wish to embrace the rich complexity of life lived through multiple and contradictory discourses. (Davis 1997, p. 272)

In this respect, feminist post-structuralism allows for a plurality of perspectives, for individuality to be acknowledged and for the '*establishment of truth*' (Foucault 1977, p. 184) to be explored simultaneously. Both philosophies also consider how people internalise these societal norms, further adding to this regulation. Whilst Foucault (1977) contests the idea that all power relations are negative and unproductive, his post-structuralist underpinning still stresses the importance of exploring such relations. With this in mind, McNay (1992) suggests that Foucault's ideas on power relations have:

> provided feminists with a useful analytical framework to explain how women's experience is impoverished and controlled within certain culturally determined images of feminine sexuality. (McNay 1992, p. 3)

This naturalisation of certain images of women, in particular mothers, therefore, can be considered through both feminist and post-structuralist lenses. By exploring the ways in which particular normalised behaviours are formed which have moved towards a specific 'parenting culture' (Furedi 2008; Lee et al. 2014) it may be possible to consider and challenge the different levels of surveillance that lead a mother to feel that they are not 'good enough' (Winnicott 1964; Currie 2008) as a '*fictitious atom of an ideological representation of society*' (Foucault 1977, p. 194). Through a feminist post-structuralist lens, I considered the constructs of motherhood whilst also acknowledging the possibility of '*autonomy and self-realization*' (Rose 1999, p. viii). Weedon (1997)

Feminist Post-Structuralist Worldview

Post- Structuralism - Disciplinary Technologies and Panoptism (Foucault, 1975; Rose, 1999);

Levels of Surveillance (Henderson *et al.*, 2010)

Feminism - Contested Ideologies of Motherhood (Hay, 1996; Douglas and Michaels, 2005; Beaupre Gillespie and Schwartz Temple, 2011)

Feminist Post-Structuralism - *'Productive Contradiction'* (Baxter, 2003, p. 2; Davis, 1997; Weedon, 1997)

Fig. 2.1 Feminist post-structuralist worldview

suggests that through this feminist post-structuralist lens it is possible to analyse the discursive practices in order to explore the power relations and structures within them, it is through this exploration that we may challenge practices and consider ways to make changes and transformations.

Summary

This chapter explored the underpinning worldview within this research including insight into why the approach could not align purely to a post-structuralist worldview. A combined feminist post-structuralist worldview (the key literature of which is highlighted in Figure 2.1) would provide a lens in which to consider the experiences of new mothers. This began with an exploration of the dominant discourses within the literature and research surrounding experiences of motherhood.

References

Ahall, L. (2012). Motherhood, Myth and Gendered Agency in Political Violence. *International Feminist Journal of Politics, 14*(1), 103–120.

Baxter, J. (2003). *Positioning Gender in Discourse: A Feminist Methodology*. Hampshire: Palgrave Macmillan.

Beaupre Gillespie, B., & Schwartz Temple, H. (2011). *Good Enough Is the New Perfect*. Toronto: Harlequin.

Clarke, B., Younas, F., Project Team and Family Kids and Youth. (2017). *Helping Parents to Parent*. London: Social Mobility Commission.

Currie, J. (2008). Conditions Affecting Perceived Coping for New Mothers, Analysis of a Pilot Study, Sydney, Australia. *International Journal of Mental Health Promotion, 10*(3), 34–41.

Davis, A. (2012). *Modern Motherhood: Women, Family and England 1945–2000*. Manchester: Manchester University Press.

Davis, B. (1997). The Subject of Post-structuralism: A Reply to Alison Jones. *Gender and Education, 9*(3), 271–283.

Douglas, S. J., & Michaels, M. M. (2005). *The Mommy Myth: The Idealization of Motherhood and How It Has Undermined All Women*. New York: Free Press.

Dreyfus, H. L., & Rabinow, P. (1982). *Michael Foucault: Beyond Structuralism and Hermeneutics*. London: Harvester Wheatsheaf.

Foucault, M. (1977). *Discipline and Punish: The Birth of the Prison*. London: Penguin.

Furedi, F. (2008). *Paranoid Parenting: Why Ignoring the Experts May be Best for Your Child*. Wiltshire: Continuum.

Hays, S. (1996). *The Cultural Contradictions of Motherhood*. London: Yale University Press.

Henderson, A., Harmon, S., & Houser, J. (2010). A New State of Surveillance: Applying Michael Foucault to Modern Motherhood. *Surveillance and Society, 7*(3/4), 231–247.

Johnson, S., Williamson, I., Lyttle, S., & Leeming, D. (2009). Expressing Yourself: A Feminist Analysis of Talk Around Expressing Breast Milk. *Social Science and Medicine, 69*, 900–907.

Kerrick, M., & Henry, R. L. (2016). 'Totally in Love': Evidence of a Master Narrative for How New Mothers Should Feel About Their Babies. *Sex Roles, 76*(1), 1–16.

Lee, E., Bristow, J., Faircloth, C., & Macvarish, J. (2014). *Parenting Culture Studies*. London: Palgrave Macmillan.

Letherby, G. (2003). *Feminist Research in Theory and Practice*. Buckingham: Open University Press.

McCann, C. R., & Kim, S.-K. (2017). *Feminist Theory Reader* (4th ed.). London: Routledge.

McNay, L. (1992). *Foucault and Feminism*. London: Polity Press.

Miller, T. (2005). *Making Sense of Motherhood: A Narrative Approach.* Cambridge: Cambridge University Press.

Rabinow, P. (1991). *The Foucault Reader: An Introduction to Foucault's Thought.* London: Penguin.

Ramazanoglu, C. (1993). *Up Against Foucault: Explorations of Some Tensions Between Foucault and Feminism.* London: Routledge.

Rose, N. (1999). *Governing the Soul: The Shaping of the Private Self* (2nd ed.). London: Free Association Books.

Weedon, C. (1997). *Feminist Practice and Poststructuralist Theory* (2nd ed.). Oxford: Blackwell.

Winnicott, D. (1964). *The Child, the Family and the Outside World.* London: Penguin Books.

3

Emotions, 'Expert' Advice and Support in the Early Days of Motherhood

Introduction

This chapter will explore historical child-rearing philosophies and trends relating to expert advice including parenting gurus, baby manuals and parenting websites with links to social construction. This begins with Davis (2012) and a consideration of her book '*Modern Motherhood: Women and Family in England 1945–2000*' which investigated the effects of the exposure to the many conflicting notions of the best way to care for children, across generations.

This chapter will also provide insight into social media as the rising 'expert' and explore the rising trend in 'blogging' versus social media platforms with an exploration of research relating to the impact on maternal mental health. Within modern society, the feeling of being scrutinised and judged within 'structural surveillance' (Henderson et al. 2010) has been exacerbated by the increase in surveillance opportunities through social networking, including social media sites, e.g. Facebook (2004), online parenting forums, e.g. Mumsnet (2000), and group messaging opportunities, e.g. WhatsApp (2009). It is important to consider the role that these popular cultural platforms may have on the lives of modern mothers.

© The Author(s) 2020
H. Simmons, *Surveillance of Modern Motherhood*,
https://doi.org/10.1007/978-3-030-45363-3_3

Extracts from the reflections of participants will focus on the navigation of the transition to motherhood and insight into the forms of advice and support accessed by new mothers during this time.

Historical Discourse of Expert Advice

Based upon 160 oral history interviews, Davis (2012) investigated the effects of the exposure to the many conflicting notions of the best way to care for children. It is clear from her research that this is by no means a new phenomenon and the accounts of the women that Davis spoke to show the level of confusion and uncertainty produced through the conflicting advice that they received from baby and childcare manuals. At least since post Second World War Britain, women have been exposed to the many different opinions on the best way to bring up their children. These opinions and a now deeply and ever-growing embedded societal perception of motherhood as a role that must be taught, has increased the potential for both the *'professionalisation'* (Furedi 2008, p. 180) and *'problematization'* (Rose 1999, p. xi) of modern motherhood.

On reviewing historical child-rearing philosophies, Davis states that *'their advice was by no means consistent and mothers were under pressure to conform to conflicting models of care'* (2012, p. 112). Her study focuses on 6 popular figures of 'authority on child development' from post-World War Two. They were Fredrick Truby-King, John Bowlby, Donald Winnicott, Benjamin Spock, Penelope Leach and Gina Ford. Their approaches range from the strict and rigid routine-based approaches of Truby-King and Ford to the more instinct promoting and baby-led philosophies of Winnicott and Spock. All held their own perspectives on the best way to child-rear based on their own experiences and knowledge which varied greatly.

Similarly, Kinser (2010) explored the varied perspectives of child-rearing experts in America in relation to social construction. Kinser observed how pressures on parents, particularly mothers are heightened during times of increased political attention. Kinser (2010), like Davis (2012), noted a shift after World War II whereby a rise in 'permissive parenting' occurred following Benjamin Spock's hugely popular manual,

'*The Common Sense Book of Baby and Child Care*' in 1946. Similar to the currently popular 'attachment parenting' style, with Spock's approach, mothers were encouraged to be led by their baby:

> Without being remotely distracted by any outside interests or concerns, those who spent hours talking and thinking at a child's level, those who embraced the constant emotional work on top of this physical work of mothering, would produce happy, well-adjusted citizens. (Kinser 2010, p. 65)

Similarities can be drawn here with Spock's child-rearing philosophy and current parenting education programmes, both of which lay the foundation of well-rounded, securely attached individuals firmly with parents, particularly mothers. Although no definitive definition is provided regarding what would constitute 'middle class', Kinser goes further with her arguments to suggest that child-rearing philosophies such as those put forward by Spock are largely aimed at middle-class mothers since '*dominant culture is more invested in the middle class in general, and in its members as consumers in particular, it was middle class mothers who bore the brunt of critique*' (Kinser 2010, p. 65).

Correspondingly, from the women Davis (2012) interviewed in the UK, she also found links to the social, cultural and political constructs of the time in which each particular child-rearing philosophy was developed. In the 1940s Truby-King's popularity was at its highest with the belief that strict routines and lots of fresh air was the key to good child rearing. The popularity of Truby-King continued into the 1980s although, according to Davis, some of his advice, particularly in relation to not 'spoiling' a baby with too much attention, specifically leaving them to cry was beginning to be seen as outdated. The rise in the popularity of the 'expert' is further explored through the work of Cunningham (2012) who, through his presentation of the history of childhood in Britain over the last 100 years, considers the importance that the particular political landscape has in driving forward a specific child-rearing philosophy:

It came to be thought that the personality type that would emerge from a
Truby-King type upbringing, with its stress on obedience, would be more
suited to the German Third Reich than a country fighting for democracy.
(Cunningham 2012, p. 202)

Interestingly, although Truby-King's strict routine-based, no-nonsense
approach was beginning to be seen as outdated by the 1970s and 1980s,
the popularity of a similar approach from Ford has risen since the release
of her book '*The Contented Little Baby Book*' first released in 1999. Her
strategies, once followed promise results including, a baby that will sleep
better, eat better and be in overall better health. Ford states that by
following her routines, parents will be able to '*understand his needs and
meet them quickly and confidently*' (Ford 2002, p. 37). Ford's book, whilst
controversial, has proven to be very popular with its promise of more
sleep for both parents and baby resulting in thousands of copies being
sold in the UK. Whilst the strict routine may return control to some
parents when they need it the most, Asher (2012) through her interviews
with mothers, expressed concerns over the rise in guilt and the sense of
failure that such advice manuals transmit:

I remember agonising over the fact that my baby insisted on sleeping after
being fed rather than engaging in rigorous mini-gym exercise as favoured
by Tracy (Hogg), and hanging my head in shame when I didn't get it
together to express milk by seven o'clock in the morning, as advised by
Gina (Ford). (Asher 2012, p. 71)

From a historical perspective, Ford's approach to parenting is an extreme
version of parenting advice. Paediatrician and psychoanalyst Winnicott
(1896–1971) '*advocated a less authoritarian and regimented approach*'
(Davis 2012, p. 119); it would therefore be interesting to consider
what he would make of Ford's disciplined and rigid style. Winnicott's
fundamental belief about parenting, specifically motherhood, is that '*best
mothering comes out of natural self-reliance*' (Winnicott 1964, p. 9) and
that, whilst there is a place for supporting mothers to reflect on their
parenting skills, it must not come at the cost of spoiling any natural
instinct. Winnicott's knowledge of babies and children from a medical
and psychoanalytical perspective gave him a unique approach to both

childhood and parenting. A firm believer in the 'good enough' approach, he encouraged mothers to spend time getting to know their babies and respond to them as individuals, and yet not agonise if they 'got it wrong'. When relating Winnicott's philosophy to modern motherhood, Beaupre Gillespie and Schwartz Temple (2011) acknowledge that his work can be considered alongside current, intensive motherhood and helpful in the realisation that mothers who '*allow her child to separate, problem-solve and even experience discomfort bestow greater gifts than the outwardly 'perfect' mother, who stifles independence by fixing every problem immediately*' (Beaupre Gillespie and Schwartz Temple 2011, p. 12).

Winnicott's approach could not have been further from the Hogg (2001) or Ford (2002) perspective of following a formula or deciding what 'type' of baby you have: '*angel baby, textbook baby, touchy baby*' (Hogg 2001, pp. 29–32). Winnicott (1964) encouraged mothers to stand back and consider the bond they have with their baby, from inside the womb and beyond, he aimed to empower mothers to trust their own instincts as the only people who really know this new person. Winnicott's approach was practical and information giving rather than judgemental or opinion-based advice, as opposed to a rigid philosophy of child rearing which encourages mothers to follow a prescriptive formula:

> One might ask how a mother can learn about being a mother in any other way than by taking full responsibility? If she does what she is told, she has to go on doing as she is told, and to improve she can only choose somebody better to tell her what to do. But if she is feeling free to act in the way that comes naturally to her, she grows in the job. (Winnicott 1964, p. 25)

This notion of 'natural' motherhood in itself though, does potentially put pressure on mothers who are anxious and struggling to find this instinct within themselves. It is acknowledged by Davis (2012, p. 120) that Winnicott's claim that '*being a mother of a small baby should be all absorbing for a woman*', could move to reinforce an unhelpful, homogenous ideology of motherhood. This critique is further supported through the work of Rose (1999, p. 207) who explores, through a historical examination of the development expert advice, how Winnicott's work was concerned with '*the pathology of the normal child and the therapy carried out by the normal mother*', which she does by '*simply by being devoted to her infant*'. Whilst acknowledging the '*great humanity and sensitivity*' (Rose 1999, p. 207) in Winnicott's work, the normalisation of this ideology of motherhood does not help to ease feelings of pressure for women to struggle to meet it or do not want to.

Mothers that struggle to conform to this ideology turn to other forms of advice as support and whilst, if we accept that all forms of advice come with a well-meaning intention, problems arise, as Goodwin (2007, p. 5) states as '*it tends to come with an ideological sting in its tail*'. Whether advice is offered in relation to how the baby should sleep, be fed or be held, conflicting opinions may leave a mother feeling confused, anxious and guilty for 'failing' in some way and thus adding to the impact of motherhood ideologies (Hays 1996; Douglas and Michaels 2005; Beaupre Gillespie and Schwartz Temple 2011) that are embedded within contemporary society.

Throughout modern history, the focus of child rearing and the impact of the debates stemming from the particular experts of the day have, according to Cunningham (2012, p. 199), firmly placed '*the spotlight on the family*'. This, according to Burman (2008) has developed as a response to the rise in attention to the importance of attachment in mother–child relationships, following on from the work of Bowlby (1907–1990) after World War II. Burman (2008, p. 139) associates this to a '*developmental psychological discourse*' which served and continues to serve as a system that '*reinscribes the regulation of women as mothers*'.

Similarly, Humphries and Gordon (1993) in their exploration of parenthood experiences between 1900–1950 recognise a shift in attention onto parenting, from a '*private activity best left to the instincts and intuition of the mother*' (Humphries and Gordon 1993, p. 49) to a '*matter of major public and national importance*' (Humphries and Gordon 1993, p. 49) with a rise in baby manuals, health visitors and more than 3500 infant welfare centres by the late 1930s (Humphries and Gordon 1993). This can be considered again in relation to the way developmental psychology, according to Burman (2008, p. 139) has regulated aspects of motherhood as it '*homogenises normality and pathologies difference*'.

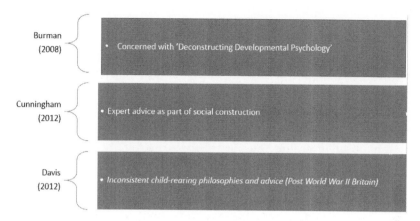

Fig. 3.1 Key literature within 'historical discourse of expert advice'

With no agreed body of knowledge for parenting practice, but with what Foucault would describe as a *'normalizing judgement'* (Foucault 1977, p. 184) deeply embedded into the various forms of available advice, the potential for feeling scrutinised and judged as a parent is ever-present with *'parents bound into the language and evaluations of expertise at the very moment they are assured of their freedom and autonomy'* (Rose 1999, p. 208). The key literature within this discourse are identified in Fig. 3.1.

The next part of this chapter will explore how the development of smartphone technology has added to the opportunities for members of society to be visible in all aspects of their lives.

Online Social Networking

Moving forward to present day, the feeling of being scrutinised and judged within 'structural surveillance' (Henderson et al. 2010) has been exacerbated by the increase in surveillance opportunities through social networking, including social media sites, e.g. Facebook (2004), online parenting forums, e.g. Mumsnet (2000), and group messaging opportunities, e.g. WhatsApp (2009). It is important to consider the role that these popular cultural platforms may have on the lives of modern mothers.

Support for such networks and forms of parenting advice come from the National Childbirth Trust (NCT) (established in 1956), themselves a key provider of both antenatal and post-natal parenting courses. They advocate the positive impact that classes and online support can provide. The NCT (1956) state that their antenatal and postnatal courses, available online or in groups, support new parents by '*allowing you to feel prepared and confident moving into the next chapter of your life*'. With more online support for new parents such as *Baby centre* (1997); *Mumsnet* (2000) and *Netmums* (2000) there is more information than ever for new parents. Critics (Lee et al. 2014) though, have accused '*Mumsnet*' and other such forums of being at best judgemental, and at worst, promoting bullying, aggressive and judgemental attitudes. Foster et al. (2003) the co-founders of '*Mumsnet*' collated many of the postings submitted by parents in relation to a wealth of different subjects. Although not an academic source, their work still offers an insight into the underpinning philosophy embedded into their parenting website which is:

> Punctuated by facts, tips and summaries of what the parenting experts have to say. From teething troubles to meddling mother-in-laws, there's not a dilemma faced in the first year of your child's life that you won't find on these pages. (Foster et al. 2003, p. 1)

Research into the effects of parenting websites and social media suggest a potential increase in interpersonal surveillance, corresponding to Foucault's (1977) exploration of 'panopticism', whereby members of society are observed and scrutinised in relation to all aspects of their lives.

Recent US findings show a tension between the way social media can be both empowering and oppressive for new mothers. Wu Song and Paul (2016) explored the influx of product information available online and how this can become overwhelming and often serve as an internal indicator to how making the '*right choices will adequately signal their qualification as "good mothers"*' (Wu Song and Paul 2016, p. 894). The idea that the materials and resources chosen by mothers for their new babies will somehow link to their ability as a mother is correlated by Wu Song and Paul (2016) to the modern-day ideology of *'intensive mothering'* (Hays 1996, p. 97). Wu Song and Paul's research explores the notion of intensive mothering in relation to the rise in pressure from a consumerism perspective and other cultural developments such as popularity in practices including baby showers, which in recent years have seen a rise in popularity in the UK and is no longer solely a US-based phenomenon.

Wu Song and Paul consider these practices as *'making natural those inclinations, dispositions and practice that are in fact culturally constructed'* (Wu Song and Paul 2016, p. 894). This research acknowledges that women with *'race and class privilege are more favourably positioned to capably navigate the sea of choices presented to them during pregnancy and early motherhood'* (Wu Song and Paul 2016, p. 895). Research by Anderson and Grace (2015, p. 943) supports this idea and acknowledges that *'social capital comes in the form of digital and critical fluencies and educational and economic privilege'*. It is not only the race or class privilege that will determine the influence that social media has on early experiences of motherhood. McDaniel et al. (2011) also found differences in the ways that mothers engage with social media to be a contributing factor in terms of feelings of connectedness as a new mother.

Exploring the rise in blogging by new mothers in recent years and examining this practice in relation to maternal well-being found that *'blogging predicted feelings of connection to extended family and friends which then predicted perceptions of social support'* (McDaniel et al. 2011, p. 1509), which may go some way to explaining the rise in *'mummy blogging'* (Beaupre Gillespie and Schwartz Temple 2011, p. 147) in recent years as new mothers share their experiences of family life. Interestingly though, the use of social media platforms such as Facebook was not found to have this affect. McDaniel et al. suggest that this absence of connectedness may be associated with the way such social networking sites operate, with mothers using them to *'look at pictures and status updates, but may not receive much support in return'* (McDaniel et al. 2011, p. 1515). The idea of reduced connectedness through social media platforms is contested by the research of Valchanov et al. (2016) though.

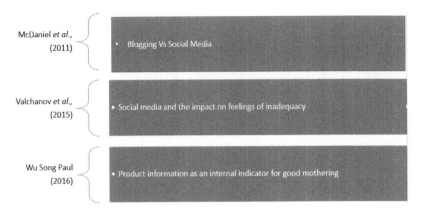

Fig. 3.2 Key literature within 'online social networking'

This research suggests that rather than reducing connectedness, through social networking mothers can '*turn to the internet as a source of community, which helps them connect, communicate and share*' (Valchanov et al. 2016, p. 51). They do, however, make links to ideologies of motherhood such as '*intensive mothering*' (Hays 1996, p. 97) and the way mothers may portray themselves publically within social media arenas and the different, private reality. Valchanov et al. (2016) suggest a feeling of judgement between mothers through social media and acknowledged varied experiences people have with this way of networking. Whatever the impact of it, a shift in the way new mothers network digitally with family and friends is apparent and the influence that those platforms have within modern motherhood is important to consider (see Fig. 3.2).

Emotions, Advice and Support in the Early Days of Motherhood

The overall aim of this research was to explore discursive practices and constructs of motherhood and this will begin with a consideration of theme 1 (Navigating the early days of motherhood) and theme 2 ('Expert' advice and support for new mothers) of the research findings. The purpose of this theme is to consider the immediate reactions

Table 3.1 Issues within theme 1

- Emotions in the early days
- Unprepared for how hard/difficult the early days of motherhood were
- Immediate pressure on self
- Frustration with partner
- Lack of confidence / self-doubt

to the transition into motherhood and how, for some mothers, this led to the accessing of different forms of advice, including the attendance of a universal parenting course.

Theme 1: Navigating the Early Days of Motherhood

This theme relates to emotions and reflections from the time immediately following the birth of participant's children. Reflections demonstrated elements of self-surveillance such as the internalisation of pressure and self-doubt in relation to the motherhood role (Table 3.1).

Emotions in Early Days

The most commonly cited words that were used by interview participants to describe feelings in this time were '*tired, exhausted or drained*' (Jenny, Priya, Ruth and Gemma) with '*shock*' (Clare, Gemma, Louise), '*emotional*' (Jenny, Priya and Louise) *and* '*overwhelmed*' (Clare, Ruth, Gemma). For example:

> Emotional. Really emotional, I think I used to cry a lot, like all the time pretty much when I came home! (Priya)

The words that were used by participants and the emerging issues within this theme related to a feeling of being overwhelmed and unprepared (Currie 2008), for the motherhood role, for example, Priya stated '*I thought I was prepared for it but I really wasn't*'. The aspects of new motherhood within this theme that were highlighted as adding to feeling unprepared related to breastfeeding, establishing a quick routine for the baby and increased arguments with partners due to feelings of resentment and isolation when partners returned to work. The words used to describe the early days of motherhood demonstrated a feeling of lacking confidence and increased self-doubt within this period, Louise for example, reflected on the early days of motherhood as '*you put a lot of pressure on yourself*'. Linking back to the conceptual underpinning of this research, correlations can be made to self-surveillance (Henderson et al. 2010) and this internalisation of feeling there is a 'right way' to parent, reinforcing Foucault's (1977) application of *Panopticon* whereby members of society somehow come to believe there is a right and a wrong way of performing and how mothers '*come to govern their intimate relations and socialize their children according to social norms*' (Rose 1999, p. 132) and if doubt is experienced about a specific role or function then they must be failing in some way.

Unprepared for How Hard or Difficult the Early Days of Motherhood Were

Three participants (Louise, Priya and Jenny) discussed how they felt unprepared for how difficult the early days of motherhood would be with responses including:

> I didn't expect it to be that hard… I just didn't know what to expect. I didn't realise that this was what having a baby was all about!……(Louise);
> I thought I was prepared for it but I really wasn't. urm, and then in pain on top of that! After just having this baby and then no-one told me about this! So yeah it was….. Not what I expected, at all! (Priya);
> A few people had said to me, 'it'll be the hardest year of your life and if you can get through that, you can get through anything'…(Priya);
> You don't realise, I don't think, how hard it'll be. You think 'It will be alright, they may have found it really hard but we'll be ok… cos we're different!', but nobody is! When you're that sleep deprived……it takes you a while to find your rhythm doesn't it? (Jenny)

Ideologies of motherhood as natural and instinctive (Douglas and Michaels 2005; Beaupre Gillespie and Schwartz Temple 2011) can be considered here in relation to how societal messages given to new mothers may go some way to explaining why they feel surprised and unprepared when the role is quite different from the one they expected. This is clear from the reflections above and resonates with Beaupre Gillespie and Schwartz Temple's (2011) research which considers that the reality of modern motherhood can be challenging '*for a generation so accustomed to raising the bar*' (Beaupre Gillespie and Schwartz Temple 2011, p. 63).

Choi et al. (2005) suggest that as within other social roles, mothers learn their behaviours '*though social conditioning and access them through available cultural discourses. However, in engaging in them, we perpetuate and reinforce such cultural norms so that they remain unchallenged*' (Choi et al. 2005, p. 169). From a feminist post-structuralist lens, it is clear that these social norms have been bolstered through attention in the form of structural surveillance (Henderson et al. 2010) on private family life for '*public, political ends*' (Rose 1999, p. 126) including the many forms of expert advice available in modern motherhood.

Currie (2008) relates the feeling of coping as a new mother to an expected sense of control that may not always be achievable in the very early stages of motherhood. This was reflected in the findings of the research which highlighted that Louise, Priya and Jenny all felt that they were unprepared for how hard or difficult the early days of motherhood would be. Currie concludes that:

> parenting is not something we prepare people for adequately. It is acknowledged as difficult, but at the end of the day there is a public expectation that parents will succeed. Future studies could explore the notion of 'real' mothering, where stress, tiredness and lack of coping or sense of control at times are exposed as normal experiences. (Currie 2008, p. 8)

Immediate Pressure on Self

Two participants (Louise and Ruth) discussed the tendency to put immediate pressure on themselves in relation to breastfeeding, having a routine quickly and maintaining an organised house. Examples of responses below:

> (Speaking about breastfeeding) I genuinely was at the point where I thought 'I can't do this' and I remember feeling like I'd let myself down and that's really hard......I was pushing it on 'M' (husband) as well to make the decision because I didn't want to make that decision. And I actually know a couple of friends that I've spoken to that have said, their husband turned round and said 'you're crying all the time, this is ridiculous, you know, we're gonna do.....(bottle-feeding)'. So I think support around that is really important if that's what you chose to do (Louise);
> You've got everybody coming to visit initially, so it's hard to try and get a routine going then and you don't want everyone walking into a bombsite so you've got to do the house and all that sort of stuff as well, so there's…. yeah, I think help getting them into a routine would have been quite useful. (Ruth)

Frustration with Partner

Two participants (Louise and Jenny) recalled resentment with their partners and an increase in arguments at this time.

> I almost resented 'M' (husband) a little bit when he went back to work, because I was like 'oh you've got some normality, and you can get up and go to work, you can have your tea or your lunch without a baby stuck to your boob or feed a baby and can have a full conversation' and I resented that a little bit, at first because I hadn't got into the swing of things. (Louise);
> 'M' (husband) and I were just biting at each other the whole time. And yeah, I think there was this pressure on myself cos I was feeding him and I had to do it and M couldn't do anything and I was angry with him cos he couldn't do anything. And expressing I just found just didn't help cos I just found that to get M to feed him I had to spend time expressing and that was just really hard work as well. (Jenny)

Lack of Confidence/Self-Doubt

Two participants (Louise and Gemma) recalled a feeling of self-doubt within the early days of motherhood, Louise and Gemma returned to this issue more than once:

> I think you are constantly looking at how you've approached things and how you've handled it…You're always looking at how you can better yourself, and I think you question yourself more than you do with anything else… you put a lot of pressure on yourself because, it's so emotional as well so its… it's a real funny one because you constantly think 'I should have handled that differently or they're doing that better than I am because their baby's…..' 'But… you're constantly questioning yourself and your ability to do this job which is the most important thing you've ever wanted… you've ever done… and you're given no instruction on how to do it!!! (Louise);
>
>   Thinking you're not able to do it and self-doubt. Over analysing everything and thinking everyone around you knew what they were doing and almost holding yourself back because you kind of felt that you weren't….. Doing it right. So you kept away a little bit, kept yourself to…. yourself.
>   H – From other people?
>   G – Yeah. (Gemma)

It is the *'idealization of motherhood'* (Rose 1999, p. 127) in relation to this notion of coping that must be reconsidered in order to support new mothers with the transition into this role without unrealistic expectations on themselves which, in the case of Gemma, resulted in a belief that *'everyone around you knew what they were doing'* (Gemma) and led to such heightened pressure that she isolated herself from other mothers that were perceived by her to be *'doing it right'* (Gemma).

Theme 2: 'Expert' Advice and Support for New Mothers

Within this theme participants reflected on different sources of support that were accessed within the early days of motherhood. Participants

Table 3.2 Issues within theme 2

- Using baby books
- Family and friends as sources of advice
- Midwives/Health visitors/GP
- Children's Centre
- Parenting forums/websites
- Contradictory advice
- Ways of ignoring contradictory advice
- Need for confidence

demonstrated awareness of added pressures through conflicting messages from these different sources of advice, they also reflected on how they came to resist these messages as confidence grew during the first year of motherhood (Table 3.2).

Using Baby Books

From the survey phase 8 (27%) of participants said they 'often' and 16 (53%) said they 'sometimes' used baby books as a source of advice within the first 6 weeks of the baby being born.

Four interview participants (Louise, Priya, Clare and Jenny) discussed using baby books as a source of advice. One of the participants (Clare) described the use of baby books as supportive and a replacement source of advice when family is not accessible. Three participants referred to the contradictory nature of such books and the way they can add to feelings of pressure:

> I do think mums need a lot of support. I think the problem with this country is, because my husband's North African and over there, they have, the family virtually live with you when you've had a new baby so you've got masses of support, and I think, we don't have that, so having the manuals and the guides and the help out there, it is a big help cos you can't always rely on your immediate family (Clare);
>
> I was given lots of books as well, who's the woman? Gina Ford..... Yeah and I just didn't like that one at all..... I felt like a total failure (Louise);

I know with T, I read too many books and I think that was, a mistake... Cos I didn't have a clue what to do and I read all these books and I tried to do everything month by month and I was like, well he should be doing this by this month and you know, that started. I think that started to stress me out and make me go a bit 'doo lally' to be honest! (Priya);

I remember reading a bit of Gina Ford and just getting a few pages in... cos a friend from our NCT course was following it and seemed to be getting on well. I read a couple of pages and her saying 'and know you have a cup of tea!' and I just thought 'I don't want to be told when I can have a cup of tea!!' and so she went back to the library! I didn't try any of that! (Jenny)

In terms of developing a sense of coping within the motherhood role, participants reflected on different support systems that were available to them during the early days of motherhood. During the survey phase participants highlighted partners, friends and their own parents as the most commonly accessed source of advice with neighbours and in-laws cited as the least accessed sources of advice.

This was reinforced during the interview phase with 'family and friends' cited most often as the place participants went to for advice in the early days of motherhood. However, it was acknowledged by some participants that other forms of advice are useful, particularly when access to family and friends is not possible. As Clare acknowledged above that baby manuals were a source of support during the early days of motherhood as she compared her experiences to her husband's culture.

Family and Friends as Sources of Advice

The most often accessed source of advice identified by survey participants was 'partner' 20 (67%), 'their own parents' 18 (60%) and 'friends' 15 (50%). 26 (87%) of participants stated that they never accessed support from their neighbours.

Five interview participants (Kate, Louise, Ruth, Priya and Jenny) mentioned family and friends as sources for advice with female family members cited most often within this category:

I did go my mum and……. Sometimes my mother in law gave me advice even when I didn't particularly seek it …. But I did use the advice. I didn't mind taking the advice, but I think definitely my friends more than anyone (Kate);

My mum came and stayed with me for the first 2 weeks… and that was amazing, I don't know what I would have done without her to be honest. But it was really hard when she went, and I found it really hard and that used to upset me loads when she went. You know, no-ones like your mum, you can talk to your mum about anything right? I did find it hard but what do you do hey? You've just got to get on with it (Priya);

My mother in law's lovely so, I think for me that's what really helped….. she's like, really supportive, she was great, so that was…. Like, they really helped me out a lot, things like cooking, you know, little things that you don't have to worry about, things like cooking dinner and doing laundry and the house they are all the extra things that you have to think about. You know like, I don't know how people do it without any, with no support. (Priya)

Health Visitors/GP

From the survey phase, 15 (50%) of participants said they 'often' and 14 (47%) said they 'sometimes' accessed health visitor support as a source of advice within the first 6 weeks of the baby being born. 3 (10%) of participants said they 'often' and 22 (73%) said they 'sometimes' accessed GP advice.

Three interview participants (Ruth, Priya and Clare) mentioned health professionals as a source for advice.

I was at the health visitor every week getting him weighed so if there was anything specific that I wanted to ask, I would ask. I think if you get a nice, friendly health visitor it's a really useful service, but sometimes you get these ones who just want you in and out or they make you feel that if you're not doing everything by the book, then you're not doing it right (Ruth);

But the breastfeeding support was really good, every time I felt down about it, I remember the health visitor would come round and she'd like literally just sit there and help me latch him on to my boob and I would

literally sit there and cry and going 'I can't do it, I'm not doing it prop-
erly!' and she'd be like 'no, no you are, you're doing it really well' and
mainly, I thought that support was really good. (Looks at young picture
of baby and laughs and smiles) (Priya);
   I had a really good health visitor with K, she was really good. Then
I joined the children's centre..... Illnesses and things like that, obviously
doctors. But normally, I'd speak to the health visitor first, she was really
good. (Clare)

Children's Centres

From the survey phase, 8 (27%) of participants said they 'often' and
16 (53%) said they 'sometimes' accessed Children Centre support as a
source of advice within the first 6 weeks of the baby being born.
   Four interview participants (Louise, Gemma, Priya and Clare) cited
Children's Centre as a place they 'often' went to for advice and support.
The importance of local provision with a multi-agency support and a
place to meet other people was highlighted here.

It's kind of like turn up (to the Children's Centre) and they ran it for
about 12 weeks. I think, since then they've stopped it and it's such a
shame cos that did, that did save my life! I think if they're spending the
money on anything it should be that
   H – it's that local thing isn't it...?
   G – yeah and even if they don't run the same thing themselves, even
just putting people in touch with people that have had babies around the
same time, cos not everybody has friends who have babies at the same
time. If you're someone having a baby for the first time without friends
who have had babies previously, it's very........shit.....(laughs). (Gemma)

Parenting Forums/Websites

From the survey phase, 6 (20%) of participants said they 'often' and 18
(60%) said they 'sometimes' used parenting forums or blogs. 7 (23%)
participants said they 'often', with 21 (70%) stating they 'sometimes'

used baby or parenting websites as a source of advice within the first 6 weeks of the baby being born.

Two interview participants (Gemma and Ruth) referred to using parenting forums and websites with '*mumsnet*' and '*netmums*' cited. Both responses referred to caution or avoidance in using these sites as sources of advice and support.

> I guess you get drawn to other things and then you're looking at the 'netmums' websites or whatever... and that's why it gets.... I don't know.... (Gemma);
>   Because he was my first, I was very nervous about using anything that wasn't NHS guidelines or anything that like that or just other people's advice, I was a bit dubious. So yeah, for him it was more NHS and midwife and health visitor websites and that kind of thing, just to get their sort of, advice.....I didn't tend to use the 'mumsnets' or things like that much. It's just too many opinions, you just want to go to one place that's got the information. And that's it, whereas if you start.... One person says one thing, another person says another thing and you're just in a worse state than you were before cos you've just got too much information. (Ruth)

Whilst recognising the role that the various forms of advice can offer in the early days of motherhood, as demonstrated above, participants reflected on the potential for confusion as a result of the plethora of conflicting information available in modern parenting (Davis 2012) and leading to what Winnicott (1964, p. 25), perhaps understatedly, dubbed '*sometimes causing a feeling of muddle*'. Priya described the experience as making her '*go a bit doo lally*', whilst Ruth and Jenny demonstrated an awareness that there can be too much information available for new mothers and that information overload can result in a feeling of being '*in a worse state than you were before*' (Ruth). As identified by Davis (2012, p. 209) with the responses from participants concurring, the sheer influx of information regarding parenting practice, with conflicting '*ideas of how mothers should behave*' and '*definitions of what made a 'good' mother*' can result in increased levels of confusion and stress with mothers feeling they have to '*adjust to these changing requirements*'.

Similarly, participants highlighted health professional support as both a potential useful source for practical advice but also a source for conflicting or judgemental advice with breastfeeding advice cited several times as a source for both support and added pressure. This is reminiscent of the work of Simonardottir and Gislason (2018) and their concerns regarding breastfeeding propaganda and the potential harm this can have on the women that internalise this message.

Contradictory Advice

Supporting the above discussion, two participants (Gemma and Jenny) also described how advice can be overwhelming and contradictory at times.

> You're gonna get advice off everyone and everyone's advice is not necessarily the right advice but I think, as you get a bit more confident you learn where... who to listen to more and what advice to take and I think, you need to listen to yourself and... cos, you're gut feeling is generally right..... Cos you think, at that point, you think everyone else knows what they're doing so you think 'oh, well I was gonna do this, this and this but I'll do it... they must be right, they're better at that than me, and that kind of thing.....' (Gemma);
>
> I think then you just become so overwhelmed with advice because when you then ask a few friends who tell you there experiences which will be different to yours and then you read a few books that will all be conflicting and then your health visitor tells you what they have to tell you at this certain point of time which was probably different to what they would have told my sister when she had her child cos things have changed. (Jenny)

These findings are also reinforced through the exploration of the rise in 'parenting culture' where Furedi (2008) and Lee et al. (2014) explore the increase in attention to parenting and suggest that the overwhelming amount of parenting advice in its various different forms serve to add to the parenting industry as a whole and promote a new myth of '*parenting as an ordeal*' (Furedi 2008, p. 97). Interestingly though, analysis through a feminist post-structuralist lens showed that participants did recognise that confidence is something that developed over time. This increased confidence, developing throughout the first year of motherhood, helped participants to resist contradictory advice and move forward with individualised strategies to filter helpful versus unhelpful or overwhelming advice. This confidence also related to a feeling of participants beginning to find autonomy (McCann and Kim 2017) and trust their own instincts more. These findings also echo the research of Choi et al. (2005, p. 168) who agree that it is only through time and experience that a mother can begin to challenge the ideology of '*women as natural mothers, immediately able to care for their babies*' and that '*agency may develop later when the woman has adjusted*', this can prove difficult for mothers in this early period, when conflicting and overwhelming advice leads to a conclusion that '*they must be right*' (Gemma).

Ways of Ignoring Contradictory Advice

Two (Louise and Jenny) participants described strategies for dealing with contradictory advice from different sources.

I think you pick and choose the subjects that were of interest to me (Louise);

It's just then finding your way; I just picked the bits that worked for us or that H fit into. If he was already doing something from one of the books I would think 'oh that's the one I'll use then cos then cos he fit into that box' (Jenny);

I think people want to share, don't they? And say….'we've been through it and it's really hard…..and this is what you can do to help yourself'. But it's just that angle of 'this worked for us but it won't necessarily work for you' rather than 'this is the only way'. (Jenny)

These reflections also relates to the 'historical forms of expert advice' explored earlier within this chapter whereby different forms of child-rearing philosophy were considered in relation to the impact conflicting opinions can have on new mothers. Foucault (1977) would suggest the 'normalizing judgement' is deeply embedded within the different forms of parenting advice, feminist theory such as that highlighted earlier by Choi et al. (2005) would agree to some extent but also suggest that time and experience offers mothers an opportunity to challenge the ritual of truth, reshape the dominant discourses and bring their own constructs to the role, as demonstrated by Louise and Jenny when they felt able to select the advice that worked for them and ignore the rest. This can be associated with Winnicott (1964) who recognised the importance of encouraging mothers to trust their instincts and recognise themselves as 'the expert' when it comes to looking for advice and believe that *'no one who comes along to give you advice will ever know this as well as you know it yourself'*. (Winnicott 1964, p. 20).

Davis (2012), along with Rose (1999), acknowledges that although Winnicott's ideas of emphasising the importance of the mother's role, could be *'censorious towards those women who could not meet this ideal of selfless devotion or did not want to'* (Davis 2012, p. 120). Davis (2012) also recognises the influence that Winnicott had on empowering women to *'have confidence in their own ability and experience'* (Davis 2012, p. 121). It is this confidence that is often missing during the early days of motherhood, this factor is considered again in the following chapter in relation to the underpinning reasons identified as leading to participants attending a parenting course.

Summary

This chapter has, through the exploration of key literature and extracts from the data collected within this research, considered the emotions of new mothers within the early days of transitioning into this role. This chapter has also reviewed some of the vast, varied and at times, contradictory forms of advice available to new mothers during this time and ways in which mothers engage with them.

References

Anderson, W. K. Z., & Grace, K. E. (2015). Taking Mama Steps' Towards Authority, Alternatives, and Advocacy. *Feminist Media Studies, 16*(6), 942–959.

Asher, R. (2012). *Shattered: Modern Motherhood and the Illusion of Equality.* London: Vintage Books.

Babycentre. (1997). *About Us.* Available at http://www.babycentre.co.uk/e10 01100/about-babycentre. Accessed 13 January 2020.

Beaupre Gillespie, B., & Schwartz Temple, H. (2011). *Good Enough Is the New Perfect.* Toronto: Harlequin.

Burman, E. (2008). *Deconstructing Developmental Psychology* (2nd ed.). London: Routledge.

Choi, P., Henshaw, C., Baker, S., & Tree, J. (2005). Supermum, Superwife, Supereverything: Performing Femininity in the Transition to Motherhood. *Journal of Reproductive and Infant Psychology, 23*(2), 167–180.

Cunningham, H. (2012). *The Invention of Childhood.* London: BBC Books.

Currie, J. (2008). Conditions Affecting Perceived Coping for New Mothers, Analysis of a Pilot Study, Sydney, Australia. *International Journal of Mental Health Promotion, 10*(3), 34–41.

Davis, A. (2012). *Modern Motherhood: Women, Family and England 1945–2000.* Manchester: Manchester University Press.

Douglas, S. J., & Michaels, M. M. (2005). *The Mommy Myth: The Idealization of Motherhood and How It Has Undermined All Women.* New York: Free Press.

Facebook. (2004). Available at https://www.facebook.com/facebook. Accessed 13 January 2020.

Ford, G. (2002). *The New Contented Little Baby Book.* London: Vermillion.

Foster, R., Longton, C., & Roberts, J. (2003). *Mums on Babies, Trade Secrets from the Real Experts.* London: Cassell Illustrated.

Foucault, M. (1977). *Discipline and Punish: The Birth of the Prison.* London: Penguin.

Furedi, F. (2008). *Paranoid Parenting: Why Ignoring the Experts May be Best for Your Child.* Wiltshire: Continuum.

Goodwin, D. (2007). *Bringing Up Baby.* London: Hodder & Stoughton.

Hays, S. (1996). *The Cultural Contradictions of Motherhood.* London: Yale University Press.

Henderson, A., Harmon, S., & Houser, J. (2010). A New State of Surveillance: Applying Michael Foucault to Modern Motherhood. *Surveillance and Society, 7*(3/4), 231–247.

Hogg, T. (2001). *Secrets of the Baby Whisperer: How to Calm, Connect and Communicate with Your Baby*. London: Ebury Publishing.

Humphries, S., & Gordon, P. (1993). *A Labour of Love: The Experiences of Parenthood in Britain 1900–1950*. London: Sidgwick and Jackson.

Kinser, A. E. (2010). *Motherhood and Feminism*. Berkeley, CA: Seal Press.

Lee, E., Bristow, J., Faircloth, C., & Macvarish, J. (2014). *Parenting Culture Studies*. London: Palgrave Macmillan.

McCann, C. R., & Kim, S.-K. (2017). *Feminist Theory Reader* (4th ed.). London: Routledge.

McDaniel, B. T., Coyne, S. M., & Holmes, E. K. (2011). New Mothers and Media Use: Associations Between Blogging, Social Networking and Maternal Well-being. *Maternal Child Health, 16*(1), 1509–1517.

Mumsnet. (2000). *About Us*. Available at https://www.mumsnet.com/info/about-us. Accessed 13 January 2020.

National Childbirth Trust (NCT). (1956). Available at https://www.nct.org.uk/about-us/history. Accessed 4 June 2020.

Netmums. (2000). *About Us*. Available at https://www.netmums.com/info/about-us. Accessed 13 January 2020.

Rose, N. (1999). *Governing the Soul: The Shaping of the Private Self* (2nd ed.). London: Free Association Books.

Simonardottir, S., & Gislason, I. V. (2018). When Breast Is Not Best: Opposing Discourses on Breastfeeding. *The Sociological Review, 66*(3), 1–7.

Valchanov, B. L., Parry, D. C., Glover, T. D., & Mulcahy, C. M. (2016). 'A Whole New World': Mothers' Technologically Mediated Leisure. *Leisure Sciences, 38*(1), 50–67.

WhatsApp. (2009). Available at https://www.whatsapp.com/. Accessed 13 January 2020.

Winnicott, D. (1964). *The Child, the Family and the Outside World*. London: Penguin Books.

Wu Song, F., & Paul, N. (2016). Online Product Research as a Labor of Love: Motherhood and the Social Construction of the Baby Registry. *Information, Communication and Society, 19*(7), 892–906.

4

Surveillance or Support? Political Intervention and the Universal Parenting Course

Introduction

This chapter will examine the increased government attention on parenting intervention, following on from the Allen Report (2011). Policies, reports and parenting intervention strategies will be explored and considered. This will include the 'Helping Parents to Parent' report (Clarke et al. 2017) which was commissioned by the Social Mobility Commission and which calls for the normalisation of parenting programmes and an increase in comparative government approaches that consider universal parenting support to be a 'public health issue' (Clarke et al. 2017, p. 5).

Insight into evaluations of parenting courses will also be given, along with reflections on the rise in attention on parenting with associations that can be made to the use and misuse of neuroscientific research.

This chapter will also include participant reflections relating to why they decided to attend a parenting course and their experiences of them.

© The Author(s) 2020
H. Simmons, *Surveillance of Modern Motherhood*,
https://doi.org/10.1007/978-3-030-45363-3_4

Political Intervention

The Labour government's (1997–2007) focus on localised support for families and the introduction of Sure Start Children Centres brought with it a rise in the number of opportunities for parents to meet in various different settings and be offered practical tips and advice relating to different aspects of parenting. These opportunities differed from 'targeted' parenting classes which provide support for parents with a specific focus, e.g. lone parents, teenage parents or parents of children with specific needs, to 'universal' or 'elective' parenting courses which are available to all parents of children within a particular age focus. Examples of these classes include the CANparent (2012) programme which is a government initiative that offers parenting courses in settings including Sure Start Children's Centres, Community Centres and Primary Schools in key areas around England. The courses offered through the CANparent (2012) initiative including Solihull Approach (SolihullApproachParenting 2012); Positive Parenting Positive Parenting 2013; PEEP (Peeple: Supporting Parents and Children to Learn Together 2014), vary from free drop-in sessions, weekly group meetings or costlier, scheduled parenting support sessions. Whether the government's initial intention or not, the philosophy behind parents, especially mothers having opportunities to meet to discuss any pressures or common aspects of their lives is arguably a positive one. Indeed, Hardyment (2007) in her analysis of advice available to parents agrees that opportunities to meet could be valuable:

> It is the isolated nature of modern parenting that creates anxiety. Getting in touch with likeminded people eager to help and share does far more good than the most enlightened of advice manuals. (Hardyment 2007, p. 305)

Support for forums where new parents can share experiences together comes from other sources. Barlow and Coe (2012) in their review of the *Family Action Perinatal Support Project* identified a gap in the support available for vulnerable mothers, particularly for those who are not considered eligible for the intensive support from midwives and health visitors, but who may still be suffering from '*mild to moderate depression*' (Barlow and Coe 2012, p. 11).

Barlow and Coe recognised the potential value for new parents to meet one another, share experiences and support one another in a safe and non-threatening environment. Their research as part of the Warwick Medical School suggested that opportunities including a befriender service and parenting support groups would help to reduce the risk of developing post-natal illness. With a rise in parenting classes offered to families (e.g. those offered through the NCT or CANparent initiative) those who wish to receive additional support through such forums have plenty to choose from. The 2017 evaluation of the CANparent universal parenting programmes did acknowledge though that '*there was no evidence of a reduction in levels of parenting stress, nor was there a significant improvement in satisfaction with being a parent*' (Lindsay and Totsika 2017, p. 1).

More recently the *Helping Parents to Parent Report* (Clarke et al. 2017), identified parenting intervention initiatives as a fundamentally important source of support for new parents. Despite acknowledging a limitation in their report in relation to the long-term outcomes of parenting intervention programmes in terms of child development, the report, which was commissioned by the Social Mobility Commission (2017), recommended an increase in universal parenting programmes and suggested that they:

> are shown to enhance parental knowledge about child development, equip them with knowledge of the most effective parenting strategies and an understanding of the behavioural tools that support child development, especially in relation to their own interaction with their child. (Clarke et al. 2017, p. 30)

With health visitors moving towards more targeted support, it is Early Years Practitioners such as those graduating from the BA (Hons) Early Childhood Studies who deliver support groups, stay and play sessions and facilitate peer group support. Edwards and Gillies note a rise in recent years in the types of settings offering parenting advice:

There has been a major expansion of state-sponsored, third sector and private sector initiatives directly targeting families under the rubric of 'parenting support'. (Edwards and Gillies 2011, p. 142)

Their research explores the notion that the advice is offered as a '*class-less and gender-neutral activity*' (Edwards and Gillies 2011, p. 142). They note that the rise in government policy and agenda relating to the intricate detail of all aspects of parenting has led to this huge surge in 'support' offered to parents. They explore whether parents are in fact '*consumers or clients*' (Edwards and Gillies 2011, p. 142) of this support and conclude that in fact the resources on offer are not entirely genderless or classless, but rather something accessed by middle-class consumers and aimed almost entirely at 'mothering skills'. They suggest that middle-class parents view themselves as consumers and '*pioneers who would like to access expert advice*' (Edwards and Gillies 2011, p. 146).

Similar to the suggestions of Kinser (2010) in the previous chapter, Edwards and Gillies (2011) suggest that working-class mothers (evaluated by Edwards and Gillies [2011, p. 14] as being *understood in relation to middle-class practices*) consider themselves clients of this sort of support, and indeed view it as more of an intrusion on a judgemental level whereby '*this sort of professional advice could cut across their own sense of common sense expertise as parents*' (Edwards and Gillies 2011, p. 142). Furedi (2008) agrees, suggesting that the '*role of the parent changes if authority shifts to the professional. The parent now has to listen and defer to outside opinion*' (Furedi 2008, p. 181). This perspective also connects with the historical exploration of childhood by Cunningham (2012) who stated that during the era 1900–1950, '*by and large, working-class mothers were less likely to adhere to the rules than middle-class mothers*' (Cunningham 2012, p. 199) and quoted one interviewed mothers as reporting '*they'd some queer ideas at the clinic....... They was full of ideas that was daft*' (Cunningham 2012, p. 199).

The research conducted by Edwards and Gillies (2011) provides insight into the perceived benefit or otherwise of attending a parenting class. If this support in the form of parenting classes or advice from health professionals is seen as compulsory and judgemental rather than those who are accessing the 'experts' advice as consumers, this has a huge implication on the perceived value and outcomes of the support. Similarly, it is important to consider the reality of the support offered. Thomson et al. (2011, p. 155), connecting to the research of Wu Song and Paul (2016), suggest that a particular age group 'consume' this advice and suggest that *advice across different media, available in a range of formats, peaks most clearly to the 26-35 age groups as experienced consumers*.

Similarly, whilst pitched as advice for 'parents', baby manuals, forums and parenting courses, according to Edwards and Gillies, are actually in reality related to 'mothering skills', this connects with the 'historical discourse of expert advice' where Humphries and Gordon (1993, p. 49) recognise that throughout history, *'babycare was seen as an exclusively feminine activity'*. Edwards and Gillies (2011) research suggests fathers are unlikely to access the support in the same way mothers will. Where mothers will seek out *'the emotional support about and the practical advice for* (their new baby)' (Edwards and Gillies 2011, p. 145) according to their research, fathers do not place equal value on such support forums.

Within their geographical research into newly emerging forms of education, Holloway and Pimlott-Wilson (2012) observe a correlation between political agenda and the movement towards normalising parenting education. This can also be considered alongside Foucault's second instrument in corrective training, *'normalizing judgement'* (Foucault 1977, p. 184) whereby through continuous, hierarchical surveillance, judgements can be made upon aspects of societal norms such as appropriate parenting, or mothering, which becomes a *'ritual of truth'* (Foucault 1977) through a combination of power and knowledge.

The Labour Government's involvement in parenting agenda (*Every Child Matters Green* Paper, HM Treasury 2003 and later *Every Parent Matters*, DfES 2007) sought to promote parent involvement and parenting intervention with an aim to *'tackle both social exclusion and antisocial behaviour'* (Holloway and Pimlott-Wilson 2012, p. 96). In 2010 the Conservative-Liberal Democrat Coalition shifted onto a focus on parenting practice and the movement to encourage universal parenting classes for all parents of young children, including initiatives such as the CANparent (2012) programme highlighted throughout this research.

Just as Edwards and Gillies (2011) suggested, Holloway and Pimlott-Wilson agree that the reality of parenting education has the potential to create tension. With critics of parenting intervention (Furedi 2008; Lee et al. 2014) and associations that can be made to Foucauldian (1977) concepts of '*panoptism*' arguing that such government agenda has led to the '*problematization*' (Rose 1999, p. xi) and '*professionalisation*' (Furedi 2008, p. 180) of motherhood, the suggestion is that current structural intervention promotes the message that mothering is a skill that must be learned rather than a relationship strengthened through time and experience. This tension is enhanced by the reactions to parenting intervention, which still brings with it an embedded stigma (Edwards and Gillies 2011) that the engagement of programmes may bring with it a feeling of inadequacy, as stated by Burman (2008, p. 134) '*how much more pathological a mother must be if she needs to be taught what is supposed to come naturally*'.

The concern that child and family policy has '*been shaped by middle-class values, with working-class parents being encouraged to behave in middle-class ways*' (Holloway and Pimlott-Wilson 2012, p. 96) is described by O'Connor (in Thomson et al. 2011, p. 122) as '*another winning strategy in the game of life*'. This can also be linked to concepts of social capital, whereby working-class families may shy away from services available to them within Children's Centres and where middle-class mothers are '*more comfortable accessing professional support and guidance and having the confidence to take what they need and want from the services available to them*' (O'Connor 2011 in Thomson et al. 2011, p. 122).

Holloway and Pimlott-Wilson also aimed to '*examine the attitudes of parents of different social class positions to the provision of parenting education*' (Holloway and Pimlott-Wilson 2012, p. 96). Their findings correlate to both Edwards and Gillies (2011) and Cunningham (2012) that middle-class mothers find it easier to accept the support available to them as consumers and that the underpinning philosophy of parenting courses is that '*parenting education is based on the assumption that parenting is a context free skill*' (Holloway and Pimlott-Wilson 2012, p. 96) and that the '*right kind of parenting*' (Allen 2011, p. xiv) can be learnt and taught through parenting courses.

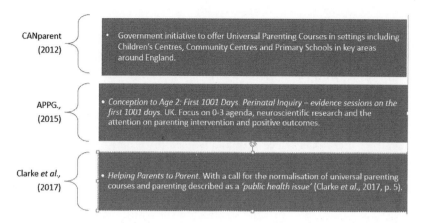

Fig. 4.1 Key literature within 'Political Intervention'

The reactions to political attention on parenting may therefore be different depending on whether they are viewed upon by members of the public as targeted or universal. It is clear though, upon reviewing the political agenda in regard to parenting (see Fig. 4.1), that government intervention strategies will continue to be developed.

Evaluations of Parenting Courses and the 'Neuroparenting' Discourse

The literature thus far has explored parenting education and the, largely, potentially harmful consequences for new mothers. Concerns focus on problematising motherhood as something that must be learnt and taught. The historical context surrounding parenting education shows that child-rearing philosophies are nothing new and although the huge amount of information available to parents on how to 'get the job right' has been around certainly since World War II, historians such as Davis (2012) and Cunningham (2012) recognise that with the increased presence of online forums and parenting courses in the local area, and with support and promotion that came from the Coalition government (2010) and the '*Helping Parents to Parent*' report (Clarke et al. 2017), the focus on parenting is pertinent. It is therefore important to explore some of the universal parenting courses and parent's experiences of these in order to evaluate the perceived benefit of those who attend them. Furedi (2008) expresses his concerns over the:

> rarely asked question – 'is this doing any good?' The reluctance to evaluate the role of this industry is all the more surprising since there is little evidence that it has helped men and women to become better fathers or mothers. (Furedi 2008, p. 180)

Whilst difficult to find long-term evidence regarding the benefit of parenting classes, it is possible to provide some insight into evaluations of some of the courses currently available. The CANparent (Parenting UK 2012) initiative held trials between 2012 and 2014 and was a scheme which offered £100 vouchers for local courses in 4 target areas (Camden, Middlesborough, High Peak in Derbyshire and lastly, Bristol). The trial was extended until March 2015 and a final evaluation was completed at this time. The pilot itself offered a range of parenting courses across the different areas in settings in local areas such as Children's Centres, Community Centres, Health Centres and Libraries. Parenting programmes offered included the Solihull Approach (Solihul-lApproachParenting 2012); Positive Parenting (Positive Parenting 2013) and PEEP (Peeple: Supporting Parents and Children to Learn Together 2014). These courses offered a range of opportunities for parents with different focuses threaded throughout including child development, play, reflecting on parenting and promoting positive behaviour. The common aims remain the same; normalising parenting courses to become as routine as antenatal classes and supporting parents with the daily realities of bringing up children aged 0–5 years.

The CANparent final evaluation (Lindsay et al. 2014) reported that the overall demand for the '*universal parenting courses was 2956 partici-pants, most of whom were mothers (91%), the overall take-up was substan-tially lower than the initial DfE planning assumption*' (Lindsay et al. 2014, p. 35). Despite the lower than expected take-up rate of the classes offered to parents; the final evaluation is mainly positive about the trial overall. Although the review is largely from a business perspective, evaluating the perceived success of the courses along with a focus on participant opinion as to whether they would have been willing to pay for such a course in the future, the report does offer some insight into the reasons behind why participants felt motivated to attend the courses in the first place, individual motivators highlighted from follow-up interviews with 50 parents included:

- Desire for parenting advice, guidance, tips
- Experiencing problems related to parenting
- Interested in learning (in general, or specifically about being a parent)
- Desire to meet local parents
- Looking for free activities to do to fill in time
- Desire that both parents would develop a shared parenting approach (Lindsay et al. 2014, p. 35).

The evaluation suggests that courses are offered to parents in a range of formats including '*face-to-face groups, one-to-one, blended face-to-face with online and or self-directed learning components and pure on-line delivery*' (Lindsay et al. 2014, p. 35). The evaluation states that the aim of the universal parenting classes offered is to:

> Increase support for parents to help them develop positive relationships and communicate better with their children, encourage good behaviour, and prevent the development of later problems. (Lindsay et al. 2014, p. 35)

As this was not a longitudinal study it is difficult to be clear as to the prevention of '*development of later problems*'. In this respect it is possible to make links back to the post-structuralist perspective (Foucault 1977; Rose 1999) that parenting is, in some way being '*problematized*' (Rose 1999, p. xi) without a clear rationale. However, the report continues to view the overall effectiveness of the universal parenting courses as positive, with key findings suggesting that:

> after attending a parenting class, parents felt more satisfied with being a parent, saw themselves as more effective parents, and had higher levels of

mental well-being than before taking the parenting class. (Lindsay et al. 2014, p. 20)

The 'mental well-being' referred to here is based upon the parents who attended a class completing standardised surveys measuring *parent mental well-being (Warwick-Edinburgh Mental Well-Being scale), parent satisfaction, confidence and sense of efficacy as a parent (Being a Parent Scale); and aspects of their child's behaviour (Parenting Daily Hassles Scale)'* (Lindsay et al. 2014, p. 51).

Although the final evaluation of the CANparent programme is largely positive, critics of parenting education courses including Lee et al. (2014) associate these programmes with parental determination which *'disregard any possibility that learning by experience, and the tacit knowledge that accumulates this way, is a perfectly good and acceptable way to go about raising children'* (Lee et al. 2014, p. 219). Whilst, perhaps unsurprisingly, the evaluators consider the programme to be a success, Lee et al. (2014) argues that such programmes have created a 'parallel universe' whereby:

> those who hold a belief in the need for parenting education simply cannot accept that parenting may neither need nor want expert advice: the only conclusion that they can draw is that more must be done to find ways to train parents and to increase 'demand' – that is, parent's willingness to be trained. (Lee et al. 2014, p. 219)

The report highlights the importance of parenting courses as a way to promote early intervention and parenting support and relates this to the importance of parenting and the critical period of the 0–3 years in terms of child development and emotional attachment. The report comments on the importance of removing any potential stigma attached to parenting education and suggest that accessing support should be as normal as attending antenatal support, this can also be associated with the recent *'Helping Parents to Parent'* report (Clarke et al. 2017) which recognised the stigma attached to targeted provision and recommended future parenting intervention programmes be labelled *'under the umbrella term 'universal''* (Clarke et al. 2017, p. 5). Similarly, the authors of the CANparent evaluation (Lindsay et al. 2014) acknowledge that there is still some way to go here and that there is stigma attached to attending a parenting courses, thus explaining the lesser than expected take-up for the classes offered in the trial locations. In addition to this, the evaluation of the CANparent trial acknowledged that despite the rationale, it cannot yet be determined whether *universal interventions have measurable benefits to overall levels of behaviour problems in the population* (Lindsay and Totsika 2017, p. 10). This has not halted the increase in the proposals of more intervention programmes by the government though.

The Solihull Approach (SolihullApproachParenting, 2012) is a programme that was offered through the CANparent initiative and through other settings and providers across the UK, they offer online and group parenting courses and training courses for practitioners. This approach makes strong links to neuroscientific research and uses this as the foundation for their courses, in particular, the *'Understanding Your Child'* universal parenting course (SolihullApproachParenting 2012).

Russell (2014) attended this 10-week course within the Solihull area and reported within the professional journal *'Children and Young People Now'* (2014) that her experience was positive, with opportunities to meet in a group and share experiences in a non-threatening and non-competitive environment, the overall experience gave her the chance to reflect on her parenting style and the time she spent with her child. She acknowledges that the stigma associated with parenting courses is still there, that by admitting the need for some help and support, parents are in some way admitting defeat:

> Signing up to a parenting course crosses the line.... Telling people you've signed up to a parenting course invites them to question the very foundations of your self-worth and identity as a parent. (Russell 2014, p. 24)

Connections can be made back to the research of Edwards and Gillies (2011, p. 141) who identified a divide between those who could be identified as *'clients'* and those who could be considered *'consumers'* within parenting education opportunities. Russell (2014) recommends that the term 'course' be removed in order to lessen the stigma in some way that parenting is something that needs to be taught. Using her own experience as an example, she now considers parenting courses as a reflective opportunity to:

> step back and observe our children. We need some structured guidance to help us reflect on all the factors that make them behave in the way they do; some development, some circumstantial. (Russell 2014, p. 24)

Other evaluations of the Solihull Approach are also very positive. Three separate articles within the Community Practitioner Journal (Maunders et al. 2007; Johnson and Wilson 2012; Cabral 2013) report positive experiences of attendees through opportunities to develop a deeper understanding of behaviour and relationships. Maunders et al. (2007) explored some of the experiences of mothers in relation to support from community health professionals and reflected on the vital role that health professionals play in supporting new parents and helping them to feel understood and a '*good mother*' (Maunders et al. 2007, p. 28). Such progammes though, do bring with them a very real concern (Burman 2008, p. 154) that rather than identifying a problem embedded into society, they serve to '*provide a scapegoat*' whereby the '*locus of the deficit*' can revolve around mother–child relationships rather than identifying where and how any real problems may have originated, in this sense, these parenting intervention programmes serve to '*negate state responsibility*' (Burman 2008, p. 154).

The Solihull Approach, whilst initially used by health professionals as a targeted programme moved forward in 2012 when the '*Understanding Your Child's behaviour*' was made available as a 10-week universal parenting programme. It is important to acknowledge that Douglas, co-author of one of the evaluations of the Solihull Approach, founded the Solihull Approach and could therefore, within Foucauldian concepts, be considered a person in a position of power who uses their position to engage in '*hierarchical observation*' and '*normalizing judgement*' as a way to produce knowledge within '*the means of correct training*' (Foucault 1977, pp. 170–194), in this case, a parenting programme, thus making it difficult for the evaluation to be considered entirely impartial.

Similarly, to the previous parenting programme evaluations, Johnson and Wilson (2012) in their evaluation of the Solihull Approach suggested that the combination of psychotherapeutic and neurodevelopmental concepts which the approach is formed on, provide opportunities for parents to not only build their own self-esteem but also understand their children better. The approach claims to use containment, reciprocity and learning theory as '*the basis for developing a relationship model that focuses on providing a containing experience for parents so that they are able to be calm, process emotions and retain the capacity to think*' (Johnson and Wilson 2012, p. 29). This research again reports positive experiences of participants with parents reporting '*increased knowledge*', '*making changes*' and '*improved interactions*' (Johnson and Wilson 2012, p. 29).

These claims would be contested through the 'parenting culture' discourse, as previously highlighted Macvarish (2014) and colleagues at the Centre for Parenting Culture Studies raised their concerns about the overemphasis and misuse of neuroscientific research by those in positions of power which serves to create a culture of '*neuromania*' (Macvarish in Lee et al. 2014, p. 166). Responses to the rise in the use of neuroscientific research have continued to develop in recent years. Garrett (2017, p. 14) explores the use of an increased '*medical model*' to suggest a correct way of parenting which is grounded in the belief that children's brains are '*irrevocably wired after the age of three*'. Garrett (2017, p. 13) states that '*across a range of disciplines, including neuroscience, many researchers question the validity of such claims and express concern about the direction of polices*', a publication from the '*Contesting Early Childhood*' series observes similar concerns about how the '*neurosciences are used to shape early childhood education as a commodity and an investment of which we expect an economic return*' (Vandenbroek et al. 2017, p. 1). Similarly, from a post-structuralist perspective, Rose (1999, p. 211) explores the regulation of motherhood '*as bolstered by dubious psychological theories of maternal instinct, mother-child bonding, and primary maternal preoccupation*' echoed further by research from Wall (2017) who expresses her concern about representations of attachment that are linked to young children and brain research within parenting education information. The way that neuroscience research is used by those in positions of power is arguably then, another form of state surveillance (Henderson et al. 2010) whereby the consciences of new mothers are manipulated in such a way that the message that there is a right way to parent is internalised. This has been further considered by Wastell and White (2017, p. x) in their exploration of the social implications of epigenetics and neuroscience. They consider this issue to be grounded in the way that it has become '*unfashionable for helping professions to accept that some people find it harder to parent and may need long-term, practical help rather than, or perhaps as well as, a targeted programme, rigorously evaluated with clear 'outcome measures*".

The final report also highlights the '*positive impact of parenting programmes*' (Cabral 2013, p. 33) with acknowledgement given that it is important that parenting programmes continue to be delivered and available to parents during these '*financially challenged times*' (Cabral 2013, p. 33). Through her survey Cabrel suggested:

> a significant increase in self-esteem and parenting sense of competence; improvement in the parental locus of control, a decrease in hyperactivity and conduct problems and an increase in pro-social behaviour. (Cabral 2013, p. 30)

Some of the above claims are unsubstantiated given that the research was conducted over the 10-week period of the parenting programme; a longitudinal study may have proved more reliable in terms of measuring the effectiveness, perceived or otherwise, of the parenting programme.

Similarly, when reviewing the effectiveness of the Triple P parenting programme, Ramaekers and Vandezande (2013, p. 80) describe an '*apparent contradiction*' between parenting courses as a way of encouraging parenting to become more independent and the prescriptive, one-dimensional nature of parenting courses themselves. Ramaekers and Vandezande acknowledge the contradiction as '*parents (apparently) can only become independent problem solvers after having actively participated in information sessions on parenting*' (Ramaekers and Vandezande 2013, p. 80). Similarly concerns have been expressed by Lee in relation to the overemphasis on the '*prejudices and imaginations of those committed unquestioningly to the importance of 'parent training*" (Lee et al. 2014,

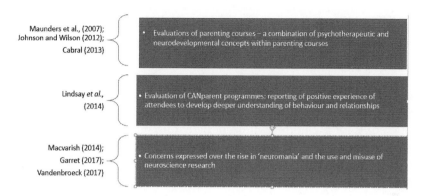

Fig. 4.2 Key literature from 'Evaluations of parenting courses and the "Neuro-parenting" discourse'

p. 220) and by Wall (2017) who contest the way neuroscience research is used by policy makers and those developing parenting programmes as a way of making '*vigilant and frequent responsiveness a necessity for all parents who wish to maximise their children's brain potential*' (Wall 2017, p. 9).

The tension between the psychotherapeutic, neurodevelopmental discourse of parenting education versus critical, post-structuralist perspectives means that there is no agreed benefit of parenting courses or agreement on how the focus on parenting on a wider scale is impacting on the experiences of modern motherhood (see Fig. 4.2).

It is important to now consider the way in which the dominant discourses work together to provide an insight into these experiences and how they will be explored alongside the reflections of the mothers that participated within the research.

Surveillance or Support: Experiences of Attending a Universal Parenting Course

The first objective of this research was to explore the experiences of mothers that have attended universal parenting courses. This objective is explored through the consideration of theme 3 (Reasons identified for attending a parenting course) and theme 4 (Experiences of attending a parenting course) of the data collection and findings.

As outlined through political intervention strategies explored in this chapter, there has been a rise in government attention to parenting education including the '*Helping Parents to Parent*' report (Clarke et al. 2017) which was commissioned by the Social Mobility Commission and which calls for the normalisation of parenting programmes and increase in comparative government approaches that consider universal parenting support as a '*public health issue*' (Clarke et al. 2017, p. 5). The report also suggests that policy can reduce the stigma (Burman 2008; Edwards and Gillies 2011) associated with parenting intervention programmes. This report, along with the CANparent initiative are underpinned with the belief by policy makers that '*all parents will benefit from support to develop their parenting skills and that, as a consequence, this public health approach would reduce the provenance of child behavioural difficulties*' (Lindsay and Totsika 2017, p. 10). It is therefore important to consider the reflections of participants regarding the influences in deciding to attend a course and there experiences of this attendance.

Theme 3: Reasons Identified for Going to a Parenting Course

Within this theme participants reflected on the factors that led them to accessing a parenting course, with adult interaction identified as the most common reason for attending a course (Table 4.1).

Table 4.1 Issues within theme 3

- The importance of having structure to a day
- Feeling isolated
- Adult interaction
- Social interaction for child
- A place to breastfeed
- Specific need or developmental reasons
- Need for practical advice

The Importance of Having Structure to a Day

One survey respondent and three interview participants (Kate, Priya and Jenny) highlighted the importance of having some structure and routine to the day with a new baby.

> Social reasons on the whole, a day and a time to aim for in what could sometimes be a very hectic week! Also met friends there (ID30);
> I liked that it was regular so I could always think.... Oh on a Wednesday afternoon I'm always gonna see these girls or (Kate);
> It was part of our routine every week.... and it got me out and it was good. (Priya)

Feeling Isolated

One survey respondent and four interview participants (Kate, Gemma, Ruth and Clare) discussed the need for support close to home as a reason for attending a parenting class. Feelings of isolation were highlighted and needing to have a regular activity. Gemma, in particular, returned to this issue several times throughout the interview.

> That (the parenting class) was a lifeline, cos it was somewhere to go for an hour or two (Gemma);
> The social aspect, that's the most important thing.... There's nothing worse than staring at your 4 walls and thinking...... and he was a January baby as well .... It was winter. In the summer you can just go out and do a bit of walking.....I remember....it was kind of like, the worst thing in the world being at home (Gemma);
> I felt alone and in need to meet other parents for company and assurance. I did not think my close friends and family would understand what I was going through but other new parents would. I also needed a quite space for my babies and me (ID8);
> I'd just moved back from Sheffield to here and I didn't know anybody and getting out, was....really difficult cos I didn't want to, sort of, go on my own. So, when I joined the children's centre, they sort of got me to a play centre. Just a small one, so there wasn't a lot of people, and it made a big difference, because now I'll go anywhere, I'm not bothered, but just

that initial get you out and get you back into the community and talking to other mums.

H – Especially when you are new somewhere?

C – Yeah, yeah, I mean I've got my family for support but sometimes you just need someone else to talk to whose in the same position. (Clare)

With an increased social and political focus on parenting education, some of the underlying motivations associated with making the decision to attend a course were explored with participants, with an aim to develop a deeper understanding of exactly what sort of support new mothers felt they needed and in some way were not receiving elsewhere. Perhaps surprisingly given the influencing factors identified by Clarke et al. (2017), the reasons highlighted by participants in both the survey phase and interview phase linked, overwhelmingly, to a feeling of isolation and a strong desire to meet a network of other adults with children of a similar age to their own in the local area.

The Importance of a Network/Adult Interaction (Same Age Children)

Sixteen survey respondents and six interview participants (Kate, Louise, Gemma, Ruth, Priya and Jenny) described the importance of developing a social network with parents of children that are the same age as their own child. Responses also related to the importance of knowing people that are going through the same things at the same time and the value in developing a social network that is long lasting and how this can become a very supportive and valuable relationship. This issue was referred to on several occasions.

Even though it was for a social thing, you still spoke about, 'oh my babies not sleeping…or have you seen this lump… do you think this is normal?' so even though you're not going there for advice, your constantly asking for advice from other people and other mums… so I suppose, definitely seeking that support from other people really…. (Kate);

I think, just a general, it's a camaraderie that you really need (Louise);

Interestingly they're not..... the people that I met there aren't neces-sarily the people that I've kept in touch with er.... But they were really important in those first few months because its... it's almost quite nice to have faceless people that didn't know who I was..... Not faceless, that sounds really horrible but...people that didn't have any expectations of how I was going to be as a mum .... Because I think you do.... Do change don't you.....you change as soon as you've got that individual and it was nice to be with people that didn't know that and.... It sounds like a really weird thing but.... (Louise);

The main thing, meeting the friends from it. The fact that it did give us help and time out of the house and the kind of.... At that point it was the highlight of the week cos I knew I had something to go to and get out of the house and I knew I was going to have people (Gemma);

It was nice meeting other mums and sharing labour and birth war stories (laughs) you know (Ruth);

Again, it was talking to other mothers, getting out, just having that adult, social interaction with other people.....I think I used to like, watching how they were with their children as well. (Priya)

It is interesting to consider the above in relation to the previously identi-fied concept of 'parenting culture' (Furedi 2008; Lee et al. 2014) which dismisses opportunities such as parenting courses as simultaneously promoting a society that internalises the belief that there is a right way to parent whilst also neglecting any *'state responsibility'* (Burman 2008, p. 154) to parents in regards to the *'provision of resources'*. Whilst this may well be true, it does seem that by considering the responses given by participants through a feminist post-structuralist lens, the most desir-able aspect of accessing parenting advice was initiated by new mothers not through a feeling of needing to be taught how to parent but as a practical self-help strategy to reduce feelings of isolation, breastfeed in a *'comfortable'* (Priya) place and to develop a local social network. This can once again link back to the work of Currie (2008) who reported the implementation of strategies within motherhood as a proactive way to move towards a feeling of coping with this new role and how the devel-opment of a social network can support this, reinforced further by the high proportion of participants (sixteen survey respondents and six interview participants) that identified the importance of a social network as a driving factor for accessing a parenting course.

Similarly, Douglas and Michaels (2005, p. 25) emphasised the need for motherhood to be viewed as a '*collective experience*' rather than an '*individual achievement*'. These findings can therefore be seen as reactions to state surveillance in modern motherhood as demonstrating a degree of proactive empowerment. This also correlates with Baxter (2003, p. 66) who recognised that through feminist post-structuralist analysis it is possible, rather than assuming oppression or submission, to position women as '*powerful, powerless or a combination of both*'. Similarly, Zimmer-Gembeck et al. (2015) reported increased levels of competence in mothers who seek out and attend a universal parenting course:

> Parenting self-efficacy does accompany positive parenting, including warmth, involvement, responsiveness, limit-setting, non-punitive caregiving, and efforts to enhance parenting skills through attending formal parenting education and self-education. (Zimmer-Gembeck et al. 2015, p. 1425)

The above research is however, also reminiscent of the parenting course evaluations explored within the literature review whereby, those associated with the creation of courses, with psychotherapeutic and neurodevelopmental concepts embedded within them, suggest an increased '*sense of competence and parental locus of control*' (Cabral 2013, p. 30).

It does seem a contradiction in terms to suggest an increase in independence through exposure to manualised and formulaic support such as parenting courses. An explanation for this could relate back to '*hierarchical observation*' (Foucault 1977, p. 170), '*structural surveillance*' (Henderson et al. 2010, p. 232) and critics of the rise in 'parenting culture'. Returning to Macvarish (Macvarish in Lee et al. 2014, p. 166) for example, who associates the increased focus on parenting practice as being directly linked to '*neuromania*' whereby the government promotion of parenting intervention programmes stem from a belief that all antisocial behaviour is a direct result of poor parenting practice with very young children. This association is explored further through concerns raised by Burman (2008), Garrett (2017), Vandenbroek et al. (2017) and Wastell and White (2017), all of whom highlight the perceived misuse of neuroscience research by those in a position of power. Rose (1999, p. 123) labels childhood as the '*most intensively governed sector*' with the attention on child rearing being linked '*in thought and practice to the destiny of the nation and the responsibilities of the state*' (Rose 1999, p. 123). The internalisation of these messages therefore leads to a misguided belief that parenting can be improved through being taught how to get the job right and ultimately produce upstanding members of society. As highlighted previously, this then serves to '*neglect state responsibility*' (Burman 2008, p. 154), with policy makers and government having to do little to address any inequalities by simply laying any societal problems firmly in the hands of mothers.

Social Interaction for Child

Three survey respondents and one interview participant (Priya) highlighted the importance of social interaction between the children as a reason for attending a parenting class.

> To teach my child social skills (ID74);
> Thought would be an enjoyable activity to do with my child (ID79);
> It was nice for them, for the kids to be around other kids. (Pauses and looks at picture of T) - I used to feel like they'd remember kids they used to see regularly. I'd be like 'arhhh, they remember, they know who they are now.....'. (Priya)

A Place to Breastfeed

One participant (Priya) identified 'a place to breastfeed' as a reason for attending a parenting class. This point was raised on two occasions by Priya.

> Because I was breastfeeding, I never felt that comfortable going out... so going to Sure Start I felt comfortable. I knew that was one place I could

go, and have that bit of interaction, feed and not have to worry about any of that? H – Do you mean the self-conscious side? P – Yeah, absolutely. (Priya)

A Specific Developmental Reason

Three survey respondents and one interview participant (Clare) referred twice to a specific developmental aspect of parenting as a reason for attending a parenting course.

> To help me be a better parent (ID8):
>   Concerns over my son having delays in development with regards to hearing and communicating (ID88);
>   I was struggling with their behaviour but after the course I realised, it wasn't their behaviour, it was probably mine. So yeah, I was looking for advice on …. tantrum twos, whatever you call it! And just trying to give attention to both of them while I've got one that's having tantrums, and one that's still needy (Clare);
>   Mainly just child behaviour and how to handle situations and going back to the basics….. we had the pyramid, where you go back to the basics where you play, talk and listen and that sort of thing. I thought the course……some of the parts of courses were for older children, not for mine, but it did give me some of the right ideas of what to do. And it does work, sitting and playing with them and giving that bit of attention. (Clare)

It must be acknowledged again though that participants did not all demonstrate quite the docile (Foucault 1977) need to be taught how to parent from a desire to increase knowledge in neuroscientific aspects of their child's development. There certainly was a deeper desire to build informed knowledge in relation to the practical aspects of caring for children. Linking to some of the findings highlighted in the '*Helping Parents to Parent*' report (Clarke et al. 2017) for example, Gemma reported '*I just wanted to know what to do with various bits, wanted advice with teething, sleeping, then subsequently weaning and everything like that*'. In contrast to this though, Clare twice reported feeling motivating factors for attending a parenting course as relating to the behaviour of her children and reflected that following on from the course, she believed that *'it wasn't their behaviour, it was mine'*. As highlighted within the evaluations of parenting courses in the literature review, Johnson and Wilson (2012), the creators of the Solihull approach encourage parents to understand their child's behaviour and make necessary changes to their own parenting practice and behaviour, this seems to have taken place with Clare who has subsequently come to view her own parenting ability as the reason for her very young children behaving in a way that is arguably, perfectly normal.

Need for Practical Advice

Twelve survey respondents and five interview participants (Ruth, Kate, Louise, Gemma and Priya) discussed the need for practical advice as a reason for attending a parenting course, reasons included a desire to learn more about weaning a baby or support with fostering a routine for a baby. Reassurance from health professionals and early years practitioners regarding meeting care needs of babies were also cited, along with an informal place for mothers to meet.

> They did weaning further down the line lots of like hold techniques cos 'I' was really windy and was… I don't think he had proper colic but he used to really really struggle so there was like, the tiger in a tree type hold…so but the, the ladies that ran it had very young children as well so I think it was kind of nice … and it just kind of put me at ease (Louise);
>
> Just wanted to know what to do with various bits, wanted advice with teething, sleeping, then subsequently weaning and everything like that (Gemma);
>
> I think helping you get your child into a routine is a big thing because I think once you do get them into a settled routine it makes life a lot easier because they know what to expect and you know what to expect, so you can plan your life more…….. I can could have done with a bit of advice with people saying to me, you know, this is a generally good time to put them to bed, this is what time they should be sleeping til, maybe a morning nap, maybe an afternoon nap…. (Ruth)

Table 4.2 Issues within theme 4

- Comparisons between mothers
- Support offered by other mothers
- Course content
- Sense of achievement
- Increased confidence / competence

Theme 4: Experiences of Attending a Parenting Course

This theme relates to the focus of the surveys which concentrated predominantly on the experiences of attending a parenting course and the context of the courses themselves. Aspects of interpersonal surveillance were reflected on here including the varied and influential experiences of meeting other mothers (Table 4.2).

Comparisons Between Mothers

Three survey respondents and five interview participants (Louise, Gemma, Ruth, Priya and Jenny) highlighted the way mothers within parenting courses made comparisons between themselves. According to responses given by these mothers, comparisons around the meeting of developmental milestones can lead to feelings of being judged by other mothers. Jenny also highlighted a feeling of being judged or compared to by other mothers when the sensitivities may have actually been her own.

> Some parents love to compare children (this is true in any situation though) (ID31);
> I did meet some overly competitive mums that made you question what you were doing but once you clock them you avoid them!! (ID42);
> The only thing is the occasional competitive parent.......but you get that literally get that from day one and people always joke about school mums you know 'soccer moms' and it's true and you see if right from day one 'oh he's so placid, just so lovely..... he's so smiley' whilst yours is sat there in a pram like, bright red screaming, with steam coming out of his

ears and you like 'oh, yeah......' and you think 'what have I produced??'
but you know, you do very quickly start to spot people (Louise);
I think there's a lot of kind of comparison ..... and I think at first
as well, when you meet a new group of friends, there isn't that kind of
trust. And people aren't meaning to be... they're just saying what their
experience is and you kind of.... They're not being nasty or not being
unsupportive... (Gemma);
There's definitely the kind of competition there, definitely (sighs) 'my
baby sleeps through the night, my baby's taking this much milk.... Ooo
look my baby........ My babies only 2 weeks old and he's already rolling
over and crawling!' 'Oh really???' (Ruth);
It sometimes did get a bit much. I actually remember someone asking
me...... I remember her saying 'oh... mines only however old and ...
and he's already crawling... oh, don't worry! You'll be alright'....It was
so patronising. It was SO patronising! I remember actually ringing P
(husband) up after and getting really upset and I think he was just like
'you need to stop going to these ridiculous classes if this is how you're
going to feel when you come out of them!' (Priya);
You do get the odd ones that just, they just want their child to be a
little bit better than yours! (Priya);
I think the times I've felt sensitive have been more about my own
issues, rather than anyone else, when I've over analysed things people have
said or done. At the time, when I was moving breastfeeding to bottle-
feeding I felt really sensitive about that......, at the time I thought 'but,
they're still breastfeeding and they're doing it all the time' and almost
feeling that they were judging you for not, and they weren't. (Jenny)

Negative reflections from participant's time on the parenting course
related to comparisons between mothers, particularly surrounding children meeting developmental milestone and issues relating to feeling
judged. As Priya reflected above, comparisons between mothers at the
parenting course she attended and her response to this resulted in a
suggestion from her husband that she should stop attending 'these ridiculous classes if this is how you're going to feel when you come out of them!'.
This echoes the findings of Henderson et al. (2010) who identified interpersonal (mother to mother) levels of surveillance as the most powerful
level, with echoes of Foucauldian concepts of the way members of society

internalise the acceptable social rules and judge each other. From a feminist post-structuralist perspective lens though, it is again important to recognise other experiences and reactions to interpersonal surveillance.

Support Offered by Other Mothers

Nine survey respondents and five interview participants (Kate, Louise, Priya, Jenny and Clare) highlighted the way that both mothers who met each other at parenting courses and mothers who they knew previously would support each other when there was open and honest communication.

> Going to a group with other new parents made me realise that the worry I was feeling was totally normal, sharing experiences/sleep stories/wind stories etc. put my mind at rest. I found it easier to deal with these things once I knew that they were totally normal (ID42);
>
> It's amazing what, just someone saying you know something like 'you look good' even though you think you've not really washed your hair or something, you know, it really boosts you and it makes you feel good......if a kids tantruming you don't need someone whose making judgements on you, you need someone who will give you that smile and tell you it's alright that that's happening (Kate);
>
> You'd go to those little group and you'd see other people crying.... Because their babies had been up since you know, 12oclock at night and.... you know... having a little weep ...and you're like 'ooooh, it's alright..... It's just such a wonderful time' (laughs). But, you know that you're totally normal in how you feel (Louise);
>
> When I went to baby sensory I remember when A was about 8 months and remember, I was sitting there breastfeeding him and a couple of the other mums used to always come up to me and be like 'oh, your doing so well.....your doing so well to still do it'..... it's so nice when other mums can tell you how well you're doing. Now if I'm out and I see someone breastfeeding, I always try and smile (Priya);
>
> Sharing advice, it was lovely. I mean, it got a bit full on at one point. When I started to get a bit sensitive about feeding or having a particular difficult period with sleeping and it feels like everyone else is doing ok and I dipped out for a bit. But everyone has had a moment and they

dipped out and then come back in and were all still in touch now and see each other when we can. (Jenny)

The findings show a high number of reflections in relation to the support offered between mothers during the parenting courses, with many positive experiences cited including Kate's reflections regarding the important boost received from being around people that will not judge her. Participants reflected that mothers do try to support one another particularly in encouraging breastfeeding and offering support through their child's developmental milestones but, correlating to Henderson et al. (2010, 2015) findings there is often an underlying feeling of competitiveness and comparisons between mothers with the acknowledgement that there are some mothers '*who just want their child to be a little bit better than yours!*' (Priya). This belief can be associated to the myth of perfectionism as explored by Beaupre Gillespie and Schwartz Temple (2011, p. 57) that, whilst this ideology may be something that '*exists only ever as a composite.... still haunts us, making it harder to develop personal definitions of success*'. This is supported within the findings from reflections of the parenting courses and will be explored again further within the 'feeling judged' section of the next chapter when wider societal judgements and pressures are considered.

Course Content

When asked to reflect on the benefit or otherwise in attending a parenting course, 22 (73%) of the survey respondents strongly agreed that the course provided them with the 'opportunities to meet other mothers'. 6 (20%) respondents strongly agreed that the course helped them to 'consider their parenting style'.

17 (57%) survey respondents offered positive reflections about the course content including flexible start times and practical support:

I joke that it saved my life but in all honesty it probably did... I'm not sure what I would have done without the support, reassurance and advice from the other mothers. More so when the parenting course finished and we grew closer and helped each other with what's normal, what's not normal and all the bits in between when we didn't have a clue! (ID27);

I think it's all practical, useful information. I've not been to anything where I thought 'where that was a load of..... you know, that was just loads of theory' you know, it was all practical things where I could take something away from, whatever session it was so with the weaning, they showed you the different stages, with the baby massage you have actual tools that you can use when they're screaming in the middle of the night or whatever and I suppose that's what you need isn't it?, because you're constantly looking for information about how you can improve what you're doing and then you give it a go. (Louise)

12 (40%) survey participants offered negative responses about the content of the parenting course, particularly about the overemphasis on breastfeeding advice.

We had a very pushy woman talk to us about breastfeeding for one whole session. She refused to speak about bottle feeding at all (ID44);

The NCT position on breastfeeding wasn't helpful. There was no information provided on other ways to feed your baby if and when it was needed. The classes should have supporting families at the heart of them, not pushing a particular agenda (ID35);

As with everything in parenting, whomever is teaching to some extent gives their own opinions. In all honesty, I feel the focus should be on empowering women to find and trust their instincts as when you do, everything becomes much simpler! (ID47)

One interview participant (Kate) noted a change in provision between having her two children. She moved into a more affluent area whilst expecting her second child and discussed the reduction in provision within this area.

When I had M (first child) there was a lot more going on because there was a Sure Start Centre just a few roads away but when I had L (second child) there wasn't much......There wasn't that many community groups, particularly council run, there was a lot of baby groups but they were run by volunteers at different churches etc. which I did attend but, in terms of the council support for our area... I think they sort of think a more affluent area.... we won't provide..... but that was something I really did notice. (Kate)

The critical importance of the practitioner role in the overall experiences of attending a parenting course was also evident through participant reflections. Responses regarding how the courses '*should have supporting families at the heart of them, not pushing a particular agenda*' (ID35) were common and often associated with how well-received the courses were and were also connected to how empathetic and neutral the practitioners were. Corresponding to Foucault's (1977) concepts of hierarchical observation, participants expressed negative feelings around the judgement of practitioners, particularly in relation to parenting decisions such as breastfeeding. For example, as reflected above, '*we had a very pushy woman talk to us about breastfeeding for one whole session*' (ID44) and '*There is strong emphasis on breastfeeding, which I understand. However, I don't think enough advice and support is given to those who can't breast-feed or choose not to*' (ID65). This can also be associated with Davis (2012, p. 211) who reported, from her own interviews with mothers, an increased feeling of '*guilt and anxiety if they did not live up to ideals of good mothering with which they were confronted*'.

Sense of Achievement from Going

Two participants (Louise and Jenny) recalled a sense of achievement and a feeling of purpose from attending a parenting course.

I felt like I'd done something really productive and I think that was a really big thing. I think in those first few months you kind of feel that you've got no..... your purpose is your baby but you've got no purpose outside your baby...and I, I remember like, M coming home from work and not really having much to tell him about... oh yeah, he's done a poo... he's done a wee... he's done so and so and so and so but... I felt like I had something to contribute to so it was a good opportunity (Louise);

I guess I'd normally feel quite pleased that I'd been out and done something and seen people. You just feel that sense of achievement for actually going somewhere and making it and if I was on time and if H slept and everything went to plan… I felt like a superhero! I was like 'I've conquered the world!' (Jenny)

In relation to reflections from the course itself, similarities can be made with the previous section where participants were able to acknowledge a sense of achievement and a rise in confidence leading to a feeling of coping and becoming more competent within the role. As Jenny for example described feeling like '*a superhero… I've conquered the world!*' each time she managed to attend the parenting course session on time and when this coincided with her son sleeping and the day running smoothly. The completion of a parenting course was viewed by participants as a '*productive*' (Louise), positive step towards feeling competent as a mother.

Increased Confidence/Competence

Two survey respondents and three interview participants (Kate, Ruth and Clare) recalled increased feelings of confidence and competence from the attendance of a parenting course and also from experience over time.

> When my children were born I questioned every decision I made, and wondered if I was making the right choices by them. The group allowed me to have a sounding board and helped me feel more confident in my parenting skills (ID65);
>
> I have learned that what I was experiencing was not unique and in fact there are other parents who have it worse than I have. I also learned that parenting is no science. It is OK to get it wrong (ID83);
>
> I definitely felt really positive after attending just because it really gave me that confidence and back up that I felt that I needed, just, so I thought I was making the right decisions about different things (Kate);
>
> Well when I first got there, I was saying oh this is their bad behaviour, but by the end of it I was realising that it's my behaviour that they are mimicking. So highlighting that and making you see the bigger picture was really good. .….So it helped me to focus a bit more (Clare);
>
> They sort of got me back out into the world, and I've sort of gone my own way now, so, I don't go there very often now. But if I want to go

back, then I know it's there, so..... So it just, I don't know I think getting back out there and talking to other mums. I just felt relieved that wasn't the only one that was going through the same thing. So, it's not just me and I felt, I feel as though I can talk to people now. (Clare)

This internalisation of the behaviour of Clare's children is worrying and shows correlation between what Foucault (in Rabinow 1991, p. 213) described as '*the regular extension, the infinitely minute web of panoptic techniques*' and the desire from policy makers to normalise parenting intervention and increase opportunities for parents to reflect their own practice, leading to an '*exercising of power, controlling relations and separating out dangerous mixtures*' (Foucault 1977, p. 199). In contrast though, it could be argued that opportunities for parents to reflect on their parenting practice is a positive step. In the instance of Clare, she felt that her children were '*mimicking*' (Clare) her behaviour, and if the chance to consider her parenting practice within a safe, non-judgemental environment helped her within her life, where she is away from her family and friends then the Foucauldian concepts cannot be considered entirely accurate.

It is important to note here that all interview participants completed the parenting course, it would be interesting for future research to consider the confidence levels of a new mother who began a parenting course but did not complete it. From the responses given by participants, the construct of filtering out unwanted information continues as participants described their sense of achievement and rising confidence. For example, Kate reported that '*it really gave me that confidence and back up that I felt that I needed.... I thought I was making the right decisions about different things*'. A number of participants also highlighted the way they began to limit their attendance at the parenting course as their confidence grew, how the course itself would act as a '*sounding board*' (ID65) and following on from it they would '*sort of carry on*' (Ruth). Relating this the 'good enough mother' discourse, the importance of opportunities for new mothers to reflect in a safe, non-judgemental way and then move forward with confidence in their role is highlighted once again.

Summary

This chapter has, through exploration of the key literature and extracts from the data collected within this research considered the implications of government attention on parents, particularly mothers. This has centred around varied experiences of mothers that have engaged with political intervention strategies, in this case, universal parenting courses.

References

Allen, G. (2011). *Early Intervention: The Next Steps, an Independent Report to Her Majesty's Government by Graham Allen MP.* London: The Stationary Office.

Barlow, J., & Coe, C. (2012). *Family Action—Perinatal Support Project. Research Findings Report.* Warwick: Warwick Medical School.

Baxter, J. (2003). *Positioning Gender in Discourse. A Feminist Methodology.* Hampshire: Palgrave-Macmillan.

Beaupre Gillespie, B., & Schwartz Temple, H. (2011). *Good Enough Is the New Perfect.* Canada: Harlequin.

Burman, E. (2008). *Deconstructing Developmental Psychology* (2nd ed.). London: Routledge.

Cabral, J. (2013). The value of evaluating parenting groups: A new researcher's perspective on methods and results. *Community Practitioner, 86* (6), 30–33.

CANparent. (2012). *CANparent—Classes and advice network.* Available at: http://www.parentinguk.org/canparent/network. Accessed 13 April 2018.

Clarke, B., Younas, F., & Project Team and Family Kids and Youth. (2017). *Helping Parents to Parent.* London: Social Mobility Commission.

Cunningham, H. (2012). *The Invention of Childhood.* London: BBC Books.

Currie, J. (2008). Conditions affecting perceived coping for new mothers, analysis of a pilot study, Sydney, Australia. *International Journal of Mental Health Promotion, 10*(3), 34–41.

Department for Education and Skills (DfES). (2003). *Every Child Matters* (Green Paper). London: HMSO.

Department for Education and Skills (DfES). (2007). *Every Parent Matters*. London: DfES.

Davis, A. (2012). *Modern Motherhood: Women, Family and England 1945–2000*. Manchester: Manchester University Press.

Douglas, S. J., & Michaels, M. M. (2005). *The Mommy Myth: The Idealization of Motherhood and How It Has Undermined All Women*. New York: Free Press.

Edwards, R., & Gillies, V. (2011). Clients or consumers, commonplace or pioneers? Navigating the contemporary class politics of family, parenting skills and education. *Ethics and Education, 6*(2), 141–154.

Foucault, M. (1977). *Discipline and Punish: The Birth of the Prison*. London: Penguin Books.

Furedi, F. (2008). *Paranoid Parenting: Why Ignoring the Experts May Be Best for Your Child*. Wiltshire: Continuum.

Garrett, P. M. (2017). Wired: Early intervention and the 'neuromolecular gaze'. *British Journal of Social Work, 48*, 1–19.

Hardyment, C. (2007). *Dream Babies: Childcare Advice from John Locke to Gina Ford*. London: Frances Lincoln Publishers.

Henderson, A., Harmon, S., & Houser, J. (2010). A new state of surveillance: Applying Michael Foucault to modern motherhood. *Surveillance and Society, 7*(3/4), 231–247.

Henderson, A., Harmon, S., & Newman, H. (2015). The price mothers pay, even when they are not buying it: Mental health consequences of idealized motherhood. *Sex Roles, 74,* 512–526.

Holloway, S., & Pimlott-Wilson, H. (2012). Any advice is welcome isn't it?' Neoliberal parenting education, local mothering cultures, and social class. *Environment and Planning, 46,* 94–111.

Humphries, S., & Gordon, P. (1993). *A Labour of Love: The Experiences of Parenthood in Britain 1900–1950*. London: Sidgwick & Jackson.

Johnson, R., & Wilson, H. (2012). Parents' evaluation of 'understanding your child's behaviour', a parenting group based on the Solihull approach. *Community Practitioner, 85*(5), 29–33.

Kinser, A. E. (2010). *Motherhood and Feminism*. Berkeley, CA: Seal Press.

Lee, E., Bristow, J., Faircloth, C., & Macvarish, J. (2014). *Parenting Culture Studies*. London: Palgrave Macmillan.

Lindsay, G., Cullen, M., Cullen, S., Totsika, V., Bakopoulou, I., Goodlad, S., … Mantovani, I. (2014). *CANparent Trial Evaluation: Final Report, Research Report*. DfE: RR357.

Lindsay, G., & Totsika, V. (2017). The effectiveness of universal parenting programmes: The CANparent trial. *BMC Psychology, 5*(35), 1–11.

Maunders, H., Giles, D., & Douglas, H. (2007). Mothers' perceptions of community health professional support. *Community Practitioner, 80*(4), 24–29.

Peeple. (2014). *Peeple: Supporting parents and children to learn together*. Available at: http://www.peeple.org.uk/history. Accessed 13 January 2020.

Positive Parenting. (2013). *Positive parenting*. Available at: http://positivepare nting.com/. Accessed 13 January 2020.

Rabinow, P. (1991). *The Foucault Reader: An Introduction to Foucault's Thought.* London: Penguin Books.

Ramaekers, S., & Vandezande, A. (2013). Parents need to become independent problem solvers': A critical reading of the current parenting culture through the case of Triple P. *Ethics and Education, 8*(1), 77–88.

Rose, N. (1999). *Governing the Soul: The Shaping of the Private Self* (2nd ed.). London: Free Association Books.

Russell, E. (2014). Lessons in parenting. *Children and Young People Now*, pp. 22–25.

SolihullApproachParenting. (2012). *Understanding your child*. Available at: http://www.solihullapproachparenting.com/. Accessed 13 January 2020.

Thomson, R., Kehily, M. J., Hadfield, L., & Sharpe, S. (2011). *Making Modern Mothers*. Bristol: Policy Press.

Vandenbroek, M., De Vos, J., Fias, W., Mariett Olsson, L., Penn, H., Wastell, D., et al. (2017). *Constructions of Neuroscience in Early Childhood Education*. London: Routledge.

Wall, G. (2017). 'Love build brain': Representations of attachment and children's brains in parenting education material. *Sociology of Health & Illness, 2*(2), 1–15.

Wastell, D., & White, S. (2017). *Blinded by Science: The Social Implications of Epigenetics and Neuroscience*. Bristol: Policy Press.

Wu Song, F., & Paul, N. (2016). Online product research as a labor of love: Motherhood and the social construction of the baby registry. *Information, Communication and Society, 19*(7), 892–906.

Zimmer-Gembeck, M. J., Webb, H. J., Thomas, R., & Klag, S. (2015). A new measure of toddler parenting practices and associations with attachment and mothers' sensitivity, competence, and enjoyment of parenting. *Early Child Development and Care, 185*(9), 1422–1436.

5

Feeling Judged: Parenting Culture and Interpersonal Surveillance

Introduction

This chapter explores research regarding critics of the rise in parenting culture including insight into the perspective that we are currently living in a culture of 'over-parenting', 'parent-scaring' and 'paranoid parenting'—this has been linked to government attention and media hype regarding aspects of parenting including breastfeeding, risk and play. This chapter will explore participant experiences of feeling judged in their mother role and how this may be reinforced through increased agenda and attention on motherhood. Issues that emerged within this section can be linked back to reflections from the parenting course itself, this includes the value placed on a supportive, non-judgemental health professional and the critical importance placed on relationships and networks that develop in early motherhood and how these relationships have the potential to impact both positively and negatively on this experience. This chapter will include reflections from the survey and photo-elicitation interviews in relation to feeling judged as a mother.

© The Author(s) 2020
H. Simmons, *Surveillance of Modern Motherhood*,
https://doi.org/10.1007/978-3-030-45363-3_5

The Rise in 'Parenting Culture'

Academics such as those within 'The Centre for Parenting Culture Studies' at Kent University have provided increased critical insight into the rise in universal parenting education. Concerns include state interference in the form of government initiatives (CANparent 2012) encouraging the normalisation of parenting classes and support in the form of 'expert' advice. Concerns over the rise in social and cultural pressures on new parents, particularly mothers, is not new though. Indeed, the work of Hays (1996, p. 97) highlighted a trend of '*intensive mothering*' whereby modern mothers are exposed to much conflicting advice and encouraged to strive to be the perfect mother whilst also maintaining a career and self-identity, has led to a generation of women under pressure from what Hays (1996) described as '*the cultural contradiction between home and world*' (Hays 1996, p. 3). Concerns have continued to be raised in other forums about these pressures, and how the increase in government policy has only heightened the potential for this pressure. This is supported with the Foucauldian concepts of surveillance which would suggest that policy and agenda is used by the state as a way of controlling public behaviour, linking again to his exploration of panopticism. Foucault (1977) considers how those in positions of power manipulate society to create rules, regulations and obedience as part of the '*panoptic machine*' (Foucault 1977, p. 217).

Furedi (2008) suggests that parenting and the attention that it has received in recent years, has led to 'paranoia' and made parenting practice harder today than ever before. Furedi (2008, p. 99) explores the different forums that promote what he considers, '*parent-scaring*' and the implications this may have on parenting. By constantly undermining parenting as something that should be learnt through the guidance of 'experts' Furedi believes the social pressures placed on parents are increased considerably:

> The representation of parenting as an ordeal is fuelled by strong social pressures that continually inflate the problems associated with it. Parent-scaring has become so deeply embedded in our culture that sometimes

commentators wonder how anyone can enjoy the experience of child rearing. (Furedi 2008, p. 99)

Furedi relates the rise in parenting intervention as giving way to a new myth of *'parenting as an ordeal'* (Furedi 2008, p. 97). What may have originally been considered as an attempt to be more honest about the daily realities of parenting as something that is not always as easy or as natural as once expected, which Furedi suggests is the old myth of *'the naturally competent parent who finds fulfilment in family life'* (Furedi 2008, p. 97) has in fact become an industry that creates more guilt and pressure on parents to 'get the job right'.

As highlighted at the start of this chapter, this critical perspective has been taken further with colleagues of Furedi from the Centre for Parenting Culture Studies at Kent University. Lee et al. (2014) commenting on the politics of parenting, raising their concerns and exploring the rise in pressures placed on new parents; with recognition given that this is usually focussed towards mothers in the form of different advice forums, baby manuals and state interference. Lee et al. (2014) also examine how neuroscientific research is linked to parenting and how this, along with increased focus on the importance of secure attachment has resulted in added pressures for mothers. Macvarish (2014) associates the rise in attention to baby brain development research with the rise in popularity of 'attachment parenting', a parenting style which advocates a baby-led approach to all aspects of parenting including breastfeeding, touch, co-sleeping and flexible, baby-led routines. Macvarish (2014) considers both attachment parenting and the recent attention given to interpretations of neuroscientific research regarding baby brain development to be adding to the pressures on new parents and she lays some of the blame with the media:

> Besides the media appetite for exaggerated neuroscientific claims emanating from university laboratories, and the promotion of particular neuroparenting styles in books, on the internet, and through parent-training courses, manufacturers have also employed brain claims to sell products to parents. (Macvarish, in Lee et al. 2014, p. 170)

It is true that many of the parenting courses highlighted within this chapter based the content of their classes on neuroscience research, for example, the Solihull approach (Solihull Approach Parenting 2012) use neuroscience research to demonstrate the importance of touch and affection in order to promote positive behaviour in young children. It is through close proximity and regular physical interaction, according to psychologists Gerhardt (2004) and Gopnik (1999) that very young children are able to form the neural connections that will build the foundations for the future.

According to such research, using recent understanding within the field of neuroscience can not only promote good behaviour, but can also help to develop and sustain strong attachments within early relationships. Criticisms have come in the form of Macvarish (2014), Garrett (2017), Vandenbroeck et al. (2017), and Wastell and White (2017), all of whom question the use and potential misuse of neuroscientific research by policy makers. Macvarish in Lee et al. (2014) labels the rise in attention to brain development research in recent years and the way this research is used to explain almost all human behaviour as '*neuromania*' (Macvarish, in Lee et al. 2014, p. 166). Macvarish also points out that neuroscientists themselves often criticise the way that this research is used by '*those who appropriate the authority of scientific objectivity to pursue moral, political, or commercial agendas in the public sphere*' (Macvarish, in Lee et al. 2014, p. 166). These concerns echo some of the discussions within Chapter 4 during the exploration of some of the parenting courses themselves ('Evaluations of parenting courses and the "Neuroparenting" discourse').

Lee et al. (2014) move on to explore other aspects of the modern parenting culture, including concerns relating to the '*breast is best*' (National Health Service [NHS] 2017) campaign which encourages all women to breastfeed their babies, a message that is positive in terms of attachment and nutritional value to children, but which does not take into consideration women's rights to choose or some of the various reasons why a woman may be unable to breastfeed. This, according to Lee et al. (2014) is another example of pressure being placed on mothers to be conform to an ideology of motherhood, with no recognition of diverse contexts and no thought to the potential harm or damage this may cause in terms of maternal mental health and relationships. Similarly, research relating to breastfeeding *'propaganda'* has also been conducted by Simonardottir and Gislason (2018, p. 1). This research centres on global advice which has promoted *'dominant discourses on breastfeeding as the optimal feeding method for infants and a way for mother and child to develop a strong bond'*. Their interviews with women demonstrate a worrying internalisation of the breastfeeding message that leads to a belief of failing in some way if they are unable to breastfeed or chose to bottle feed their baby.

Lee et al. (2014) believes that claims relating to the benefits of breast-feeding have been used to promote *'parenting determinism'* (Lee in Lee et al. 2014, p. 217). This echoes the work of Holloway and Pimlott-Wilson (2012) who expressed concerns over parenting support which does not take into account different social contexts. When practices within parenting are promoted through policy and media propaganda and the idea that a 'one size fits all philosophy' to breastfeeding, behaviour management or sleep training is presented as appropriate, the opportunity for suppression and inequality is heightened. This is further supported through the work of post-structuralist writer Rose (1999, p. 211) who claims that *'forms of parental authority, ways of disciplining children, prohibitions on certain types of activity differed among classes and cultures'* and yet, through the means of 'structural surveillance' (Henderson et al. 2010), judgemental and formulaic parenting practice has *'imposed one set of norms as if they were universal'* (Rose 1999, p. 211).

Similarly, Guldberg (2009, p. 2) suggests that modern motherhood is currently positioned within a wider *'parenting industry'* in which government policy and popular cultural genres alike prey on the insecurity of new parents and seek to rectify problem parenting. Guldberg's (2009) concerns about these 'experts' relate to what she considers the *'flawed assumptions'* (Guldberg 2009, p. 141) of what these experts consider to be good advice. Indeed, she suggests much of the advice offered could be construed as *'intrusive and patronising'* (Guldberg 2009, p. 141), therefore more connected to societal expectations on children's behaviour rather than education. Guldberg does, however acknowledge some value in providing forums for parents to share *'common challenges'* (Guldberg 2009. p. 143), for example, coping with toddler tantrums or sleep problems. Guldberg, correlating to the earlier discussion regarding the historical forms of expert advice from Davis (2012) and Cunningham (2012) has concerns that extend further and relate to the over-reliance on the self-proclaimed experts to tell parents how to parent instead of empowering parents to trust and to develop their own instincts:

> The widespread idea that parents must always seek expert advice or risk raising 'damaged' children who will then do damage to society – an idea continually promoted by government officials, television gurus and numerous newspaper and magazine articles – only contributes to feelings of uncertainty among parents. (Guldberg 2009, p. 143)

Anderegg (2003) also agrees that the notion of encouraging new parents to seek guidance rather than trust or be offered support to develop their own parenting instincts is fundamentally flawed. Exploring the notion of '*over-parenting*' (Anderegg 2003, p. 4) and how, within the American culture this is associated with the feast of parenting advice forums preying on an already overly anxious parenting culture:

> Overthinking, overworrying and eventually, overreacting on the decisions arrived at in a worried state. Overparenting is trying to make perfect decisions every single time, in a world that is much more indeterminate and forgiving than most parents think. (Anderegg 2003, p. 4)

Anderegg associates much of this worry to the facts that mothers may no longer live in communities with extended families around to support one another and discuss common problems. Therefore, he suggests that parents use books and magazines as a way of discovering if anyone else is finding the same aspects of parenting as difficult as they are. Anderegg (2003) suggests the main problem with this form of support-seeking is the media hype that can be associated with common childhood issues becoming a 'crisis'. This trend as described by Anderegg increases the anxiety felt by parents, particularly those who are already feeling isolated without extended family to support them. Anderegg suggests that '*We would certainly expect such people to be more worried about raising their children than their parents were*' (Anderegg 2003, p. 5). There are similarities to the thoughts of Lee et al. (2014) here who, in her consideration of the CANparent (2012) programmes promoted by the government, voices her concerns about:

> the belief that raising children is just too important and difficult to be left to mere parents and their communities has become a dogma, which allows no room for alternative evidence or viewpoints. (Lee et al. 2014, p. 219)

The above perspective on parenting advice in its various forms presenting parenting as an ordeal or '*predicated on the assumption that unless guided and educated, parental behaviour represents a risk to children*' (Furedi 2008, p. 104) places no value on the parenting courses, manuals and other forms of advice forums that so many new parents, in particular new mothers, access regularly.

The perspectives from within the parenting culture discourse offers an important insight into the potential harm that may be caused by the attention currently placed on all aspects of parenting (see Fig. 5.1). It must be acknowledged though that there are similarities to be made with criticisms that come from feminist arguments (McNay 1992; Ramazanoglu 1993) in relation to the post-structuralist tendency fail

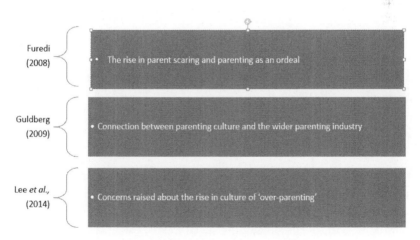

Fig. 5.1 Key literature within 'the rise in parenting culture'

to recognise that human beings may react in different ways to such attention.

The next part of this chapter will explore, through participant reflections, opportunities where mothers, rather than being hapless victims of the parenting culture, may also take the wealth of available advice and select relevant parts, resisting, reshaping or ignoring the rest. Currie (2008) for example, considers how mothers use parenting advice including parenting courses as a tool for empowerment; taking the advice they see as valuable and building strategies in order to regain some control within the new role.

Feeling Judged

The second objective identified within this research was to explore the constructs of modern motherhood in relation to different levels of surveillance and this will be explored through a consideration of theme 5 (Feeling Judged) of the findings. Issues that emerged within this section can be linked back to reflections from the parenting course itself, this includes the value placed on a supportive, non-judgemental health professional and the critical importance placed on relationships and networks that develop in early motherhood and how these relationships have the potential to impact both positively and negatively on this experience. Now, some of the wider societal experiences of motherhood can be explored through the analysis of the data collected during both phases of the research.

Theme 5: Feeling Judged

The effects of all three levels of surveillance (state, interpersonal and self) were demonstrated within this theme. Reflections focussed on feelings of being judged within the mother role, an awareness of different sources that increase this feeling including social media, celebrity culture and the parenting industry and the overriding difficulty in resisting these sources of added pressure (Table 5.1).

Table 5.1 Issues within theme 5

- Not wanting to 'bother' a GP
- Feelings of a 'hidden agenda' of health professionals over issues e.g. breastfeeding/growth
- The importance of non-judgemental health practitioners e.g. no pressure for 'textbook' babies
- Judgements from others e.g. family, friends, strangers
- Reflecting on historical parenting styles/generational differences
- Need for honesty between mothers
- Role of social media
- Added pressure of media/celebrity
- Awareness of 'parenting industry'

Not Wanting to 'Bother' a GP

Two participants (Kate and Ruth) mentioned a feeling of not wanting to take minor issues to a doctor.

> Particularly as a new mum….. You feel like…. If you're going to the doctors to ask a question, you need to ask a really serious question. You don't want to ask about… Snot or something….whereas in a more informal setting… you feel as though you can talk about anything… and it's much more relaxed and you feel that no-one is going to judge you. Whereas you feel like, yeah, if you're going to book an appointment with the doctors, it needs to be a serious issue and a problem (Kate);
>
> I didn't find very helpful whenever I went to a GP, I was sort of made to think that I was being an over cautious mum and I was being over anxious and I was, you know, taking it too far sort of thing, so I tried to steer away of GPs which isn't great, you know, you should feel that you can go and see a GP if you need to. (Ruth)

In relation to the important role health professionals have in the early days of motherhood, both Ruth and Kate reported feeling that they should avoid taking their child to the doctors unless there is a *serious issue and a problem* (Kate). Both participants reflected on the usefulness of local settings where they could go to where *it's more relaxed and no-one is going to judge you* (Kate) and seek advice on the daily queries without the feeling that they are taking a doctor's appointment over something that may be considered trivial and feel they are '*wasting their time*' or '*being an over cautious mum and I was being over anxious*' (Ruth). Whilst it is a positive example of how services can support new mothers on a local level, it is also a concern that mothers do not feel they can make an appointment to see a doctor without questioning themselves or feeling judged. Davis (2012, p. 211) raised similar concerns and also found that the reflections of mothers evidence a worrying '*arrogance of medical professionals who felt that they, rather than the women they attended, knew best*'. This finding also resonates with research identified within the literature review relating to the 'good enough mother discourse' whereby Henderson et al. (2010, p. 235) recognise modern motherhood as an experience of constant scrutiny from both '*formal and informal settings*'. Within formal settings this can be linked to how '*professionals in social institutions such as education, medicine, or even child psychology serve as social control agents*' (Henderson et al. 2010, p. 235), further enforced through the way neuroscientific research is used to make direct links between parenting and positive outcomes for children (Wall 2017; Vandenbroeck et al. 2017).

Feelings of a 'Hidden Agenda' of Health Professionals

Three participants (Gemma, Ruth and Jenny) mentioned a feeling of a hidden agenda with health professionals and parenting course professionals. This seemed particularly pertinent around breastfeeding advice with concerns expressed from participants about the lack of information given in relation to bottle feeding or support for those who are unable to or choose not to breastfeed.

> They wouldn't even teach you about bottle feeding or anything like that at all, at the NCT they said they wouldn't even cover it because that's not what they advise or what they do and I remember kind of thinking 'right ok' and genuinely don't think I would have even read into how I would have don't it because I just expected to be very, very, it's all natural and it'll all happen and your baby will be fine….. And actually that wasn't my experience at all (Gemma);

It's (breastfeeding) a big thing they try and push and I don't think previously they've understood the impact that that has on mothers that can't do it or don't want to do it. It can really knock your confidence.... And you have people ringing you up you know, 'are you still breast-feeding, are you still managing it?' and you don't want that in your home! ....It's just, it's too intrusive I think, it's far too intrusive (Ruth);

I actually spoke to our NCT course leader.... she actually said 'well our hands are tied, we can't say anything about bottle feeding during the NCT courses cos we've signed up to the world health organisation code on breastfeeding' and I said 'well I think.....the code should be about supporting mothers to be happy and healthy and....... I don't know anybody who hasn't given it there absolute best shot to breastfeed....'. The most important thing is that they're happy, relaxed and feeding their baby'.......had I know that, perhaps I wouldn't have gone to the NCT classes......They are very one sided in what they'll tell you and you'll learn a lot more... when baby arrives. (Jenny)

Although the focus of the interview was post-natal parenting courses, Gemma, Ruth and Jenny all reflected back to antenatal classes provided by the NCT or support immediately following birth where feeding advice was only given from a perceived one-sided perspective. Gemma reported an expectation, enhanced by the classes she attended before birth that breastfeeding would be '*all natural and it'll all happen and your baby will be fine..... And actually that wasn't my experience at all*', with Jenny describing a situation where she asked the course leader why no information regarding bottle feeding was given out. Jenny expressed anger at being told by the course leader '*well our hands are tied, we can't say anything about bottle feeding during the NCT courses cos we've signed up to the world health organisation code on breastfeeding*'. Ruth also demonstrated frustration towards health professionals in relation to the overemphasis on breastfeeding, stating this, '*is too intrusive I think, it's far too intrusive*'. Rather than being docile recipients of support or expert advice here, participants demonstrated a clear awareness of the potential damage this level of intrusion can have. This is another example where, though a feminist post-structuralist lens, of the different reactions mothers have to the dominant discourses surrounding them.

The Importance of Non-judgemental Health Practitioners

Five participants (Louise, Gemma, Ruth, Priya and Jenny) highlighted the importance for the health professionals and early years practitioners that offer parenting courses to be non-judgemental and recognise all children as individuals rather than adding pressure through developmental milestones.

> I remember T wouldn't have lumpy food for ages, and they would be really funny, they'd keep telling me that, he should be having this by now and he should be doing this now…. so I would find them to be quite forceful like that…. Kind of judgemental…. I experienced that with T, and I was really upset after, I'd be like 'well obviously I'm doing something wrong because he's not doing it and maybe I should be doing something different.' I learnt that when I had A (second child). I just used to… if I needed to take him for appointments and get him weighed, I would just not tell them…. just so I didn't get judged by it, and it was fine. I felt much better for it!… all kids do stuff at different stages, it's not all textbook or, you know, every child develops differently (Priya);
>
> I'd get anxious before I went, in-case they asked me something about what he was doing and if he wasn't doing it or if he wasn't doing it at the right age and I'd start over thinking things and getting stressed out about things like that.. I think if that pressure wasn't on, I think I maybe would have gone a bit more….. sometimes, I wouldn't even go….. (Priya);
>
> I think (parenting course practitioners need to be) just open, friendly. Non-judgemental and I guess that's the bit you didn't get from the NCT. She was very friendly but obviously now I know she was pushing a certain agenda and wasn't a neutral. Whereas, some of the other groups, like baby bundle, the lady who lead that was lovely and just wouldn't bat an eyelid whether someone got food out or boobs out or you know, changing nappies or whatever, it was just anything goes and that's what you want in that sort of environment, you don't want to feel that you're doing something wrong or being judged. (Jenny)

The importance of health practitioners to have empathy and their own experience was highlighted by Louise:

You're instantly looking for someone to bond with over that experience and......that's what I found very useful, when someone says....
Oh yeah, that's what mine were like and mine did this.... And 'oh god
yeah..... This happened' someone who's really chilled out about it and
also someone who talks to you... in lamens terms.....

I think sometimes, it's all very medical at certain points of your pregnancy you know, I think, when you've got someone in front of you that's
talking from personal experience and they're explaining ...... and they're
like.... Have you tried this or have you tried that??? Cos I think some
of them... I remember some people say to me 'oh, my health visitor has
told me not to cuddle my baby and they've told me to put them in a
basket as soon as they're asleep and blah blah blah...'. (Louise)

The theme of feeling judged emerges many times throughout this
research, the scrutiny and surveillance attached to new mothers is
extreme and can certainly also be associated with concepts of the impact
of surveillance and power.

Foucault (1977) described the levels of power connected to the role
such as doctors as promoting '*domination*', arguing that '*power ultimately
is repression; repression, ultimately is the imposition of the law; the law, ultimately, demands submission*' (Dreyfus and Rabinow 1982, p. 130). It is
the case here that levels of surveillance have affected new mothers in such
a way that they feel unable to seek support from a doctor. Whilst more
comfortable seeking support from other health professional including
health visitors, midwives and practitioners leading parenting courses,
there is still a reported feeling of '*pushing a certain agenda*' (Jenny) by
some health professionals and a need for individualised support rather
than the promotion of homogenous, formulaic or judgemental parenting
advice. It is essential therefore, that health professionals are aware, not
only of the important role they play as the service that new mothers may
feel the most comfortable with, but the risk factor that has developed
due to mothers feeling that they will be judged about the decisions they
make.

This feeling of health professionals having a hidden agenda around
issues such as breastfeeding is a cause for concern as it led to a mistrust
from some of the participants (Louise, Gemma, Ruth, Priya and Jenny)
who wish for individualised support not only for themselves when

making decisions, but also for their babies in relation to meeting developmental milestones. Judgement and expectation from practitioners who are not '*a neutral*' (Jenny) source of support added to the anxiety and pressure felt by mothers, the concerns expressed by participants have wider implications and can be associated to what Rose (1999, p. 133) labelled the '*three guises of normality*', whereby child-rearing practices are viewed upon as '*natural and hence healthy*' (mothers that breastfeed), '*judged and found unhealthy*' (mothers that do not breastfeed) and '*what is to be produced by rationalised social programmes*' (the support currently offered to new mothers). That an awareness and at times, resistance, to the overemphasis on breastfeeding from health professionals has been demonstrated by participants, does not diminish the concern regarding the pressure that this is adding to new mothers, even those who do not '*buy into*' Henderson et al. (2015, p. 512) the dominant discourses of motherhood. Similarly, the research by Simonardottir and Gislason (2018, p. 7) suggests a worrying internalisation of the 'breast is best' message whereby women fear that their children are '*lesser than because of not being breastfed*', despite the simultaneous recognition by the same women of the breastfeeding '*narrative as propaganda*' (Simonardottir and Gislason 2018, p. 7).

From a feminist post-structuralist perspective, other examples of resistance and challenge to the dominant discourses were demonstrated by participants. Although perhaps worryingly, this resistance was in the form of withholding any information that may be judged upon. Priya in particular noted several times the internalisation of pressure that came from feeling that her baby should have met developmental milestones at the '*right textbook age*'. She went on to report that she felt so strongly about this sense of being judged by health professionals that she would either not attend the parenting course or, on occasions, withhold information about her child's development. This finding correlates with Foucault's (1977) instruments of correct training where normalising judgement is '*simultaneously individualistic and homogenous as it seeks to make individuals conform to the acceptable standard of behaviours*' (Wallbank 2001, p. 7). Similarly, Henderson et al. (2010) report the opportunity for parents to internalise the pressure produced through formal power relationships when, '*there are signs that a parent is not meeting that perfect standard*' (Henderson et al. 2010, p. 235) and, as stated by Kerrick and Henry (2017, p. 3) mothers '*both take up and resist cultural expectations or master narratives of motherhood*'.

The feeling of being judged, and the pressure to ensure that their baby meets certain developmental milestones, seems to relate to a lottery of the type of support provided by health professionals. In contrast to Priya; Gemma Jenny and Louise expressed the relief of having access to an empathetic health professional where there was '*no…. shoving it down your face*' (Gemma) and how important that is because '*you don't want to feel that you're doing something wrong or being judged*' (Jenny). This culture of development occurring in line with a '*textbook*' (Priya) though may also be associated to wider ongoing debates relating to the professionalisation of the early years workforce (Musgrave 2010; Dyer 2018; Moss 2017; Murray 2018). The debate regarding qualifications, pay and status of those working with children and families suggests that the current early years workforce is '*dominated by a strongly positivistic and regulatory discourse*' (Moss 2017, p. 11) and that those working in the sector face limited agency, few opportunities for critical reflection on their own practice and are in danger of '*being perceived as technicians fulfilling pre-set approved practices*' (Dyer 2018, p. 9 in Czerniawski and Lofthouse 2018). It was important therefore when evaluating the findings and considering the implications for practice to reflect on the role of those delivering the parenting courses and the reality that they may be facing similar problems in their challenge to find autonomy as the mothers themselves.

Judgements from Others

Two participants (Louise and Gemma) highlighted feelings of being judged by other people particularly in relation to breastfeeding and behaviour management.

> When you take your kids to cafes and restaurants and there's like… older couples…. it's almost like they've forgotten how hard it is to have a child

...... and you get funny looks don't you and ..... I always think it's always refreshing when you come across an older person that remembers what it's like having their child and you kind of...... you feel a kind of a bond there (Louise);

It's almost like it's an Issue like 'oh, you've got to......got to feed again?' whereas when you have a bottle it doesn't matter where you feed them.... So I've, I have fed her out and about and I have felt more confident this time but with H, I would absolutely never had the confidence to do that.

H – to breastfeed in public?

G – No. I think if I'd carried on just breastfeeding H then I would have completely lost the plot (laughs). (Gemma)

Reflecting on Historical Parenting Styles/Generational Differences

Two participants (Louise and Ruth) reflected on the generational differences with parenting styles including the added pressure in relation to the exposed nature of modern parenting, greater expectations on children to conform to an adult world and changes in regards to increased financial pressures for mothers to return to work.

> I do think that's one of the added difficulties with our generation now, cos, everyone's parenting techniques are in your face. You can't do it your own way without thinking, maybe their way is better because you know, when you think about when our mums had us, it wasn't like that, and they might have had a home phone and might catch up at playgroups and stuff. But there just wasn't the pressure, and I suppose all these parenting courses, they wouldn't have been around necessarily, would they? (Louise)

Reports from participants concerning the judgement of others were not limited to health or early years professionals, who could be considered, by mothers, to be in positions of hierarchy and therefore associated with structural surveillance (Henderson et al. 2010). As shown in the reflections, participants also commented on the judgements made from other members of society and from other mothers. This was considered in relation to 'interpersonal surveillance' which was identified by Henderson et al. (2010) in their research as being the most powerful level of surveillance. Judgements made by family members, friends and even strangers, were all highlighted during the interviews as aspects of motherhood that can heighten the overall feeling of being scrutinised with breastfeeding and behaviour management cited as particular aspects of motherhood that are observed closely by others, linking to not feeling 'good enough' (Winnicott 1964; Currie 2008) in their role. Generational changes were also highlighted by Louise and Ruth as adding to the pressure on new mothers, with modern parenting bringing with it a feeling that *'everyone's parenting techniques are in your face, you can't do it your own way without thinking, maybe their way is better'* (Louise).

Need for Honesty Between Mothers

Four participants (Kate, Louise, Ruth and Priya) discussed the need for more honesty between mothers rather than a feeling of having to hide the challenges that this role brings.

> We were just saying to each other 'oh yeah, everything's great!' and actually, we said let's stop doing that and say 'I've had a rubbish week! Works been really hard, M has been playing up and having tantrums, M is not sleeping' and let's just say to each other what our… issues have been that week because it makes us feel, actually better, because instead of trying to perform as 'supermum'…. because it is very easy to go 'oh everything's great' but actually deep down you're thinking 'ahhhhh, help!' (Kate);
> I suppose it's only really after those first few weeks that people start being honest and saying 'oh my god…' and don't get me wrong you do still get people that you come across that say 'oh yeah, they're sleeping through at 4 days old' and you're like 'hahaha…. Ok!' but I would say …. Once I'd found …the people that I was comfortable with and I felt people I knew were telling the truth…. (Louise);
> Unless its mothers who are already your friends and you just happen to have had babies at the same time. I think that's the best kind of support you can get because, you're gonna be honest with each other… about the horrors! (Laughs). Whereas other mothers…… (see) their child through rose tinted glasses and you need someone… …….If you've got friends that are honest…. it really makes a difference because… its, it can be hilarious! Some of the things that you talk about, but I don't think other

mums have got that level of honesty. Probably because there is so much pressure around to be....this super-mum. You know, your child's the best behaved, best dressed, your house is the cleanest, your full face of makeup and hair done by 8 o'clock in the morning and full-time job.... And it's not, it's not realistic (Ruth);

Although sometimes I think a lot of the time... people..... Lie! A lot of the time, I've now figured that out! Back then I think you just feel that...oh god... their kids do this and they do this but my kids don't but I've now come to believe that they lie! (Priya)

It seems that, on a wider scale, more acknowledgement of the daily realities and difficulties of parenting need to be expressed between mothers rather than a feeling of projecting a perfect ideology that has '*driven us to strive for maternal superstardom*' (Beaupre Gillespie and Schwartz Temple (2011, p. 57) and viewing motherhood through '*rose tinted glasses*' (Ruth). Participants, in these reflections, highlighted a feeling of having to hide the challenges that modern motherhood brings and how, when a connection is found with another mother and honest reflections are made, this brings with it a level of support and reprieve. Kate reflects above, on an experience when she and her friend acknowledged they were '*trying to perform as supermum*', and not being honest with each other, '*we realised that we were just saying to each other 'oh yeah, everything's great!' and actually, we said let's stop doing that*'. Similarly, Ruth noted that when friends are honest with each other '*it can be hilarious!*' with Louise emphasising the importance of finding a network that '*I knew were telling the truth*'.

Role of Social Media

Three participants (Kate, Louise and Gemma) all mention the role that social media plays in adding pressure to motherhood.

Everything is so highlighted these days....everything is either on Facebook or... I do think it's because there is so much opportunity now to interact with each other... because our phones are so readily available and we have these apps you know, what's app and viber and we create these groups and you know, it can turn into a bit of a monster really, that gets bigger than you need it to be (Kate);

I think what makes parenting is very different these days, like with the whole Facebook thing and social media thing.... people put snapshots and snippets.... The best bits and you don't see the rest of it and I think, if you're someone that does worry and constantly thinks, is my child happy? You would question it because you think..... well their child is always happy.... But there are things that they don't tell you about. And M (husband)......can spot people like that straight away, whereas I'm not like that..... I'm crying inside! But you do start to get used to it don't you, and you start to realise the truth don't you, cos you know that it can't be perfect all the time! (Louise);

I've had weeks where I don't look at Facebook and you actually feel well... happier... you don't have that constant 'what are people doing?' ....if you're just at home and kind of pottering around. You don't have that 'oh, they're travelling, they're doing that' .....you can't get away from it can you? And generally people put the best of what they're doing on it and you're thinking 'oh my god, people are living the best all the time' and they're perhaps not and perhaps they're just doing that once in a lifetime, but you don't know that.....but you just think 'oh, that's what they're doing and that's what their lifestyle is like' and you just think 'oh, I'm just here and I'm stuck in xxxx and wah wah wah' ...... so I find that... getting away from Facebook sometimes, that helps. (Gemma)

The above reflections correlate with the work of Hays (1996) high-lighted within the literature review regarding how modern motherhood promotes '*the ideology of intensive mothering and the extent to which mothers' attempts to live up to it is responsible for the cultural contradictions of motherhood*' (Hays 1996, p. 97). This can be further supported by returning to Henderson et al. (2010) and their suggestion that interpersonal surveillance is the most powerful level of surveillance for mothers, and Foucault's (1977) proposal that the panoptic machine includes all members of society, not just those in positions of hierarchy. This also relates to Rose (1999, p. 133) and his suggestion that there are a set of '*instructions to all involved as to how they should identify normality and conduct themselves in a normal fashion*'. Thus, the way that mothers compare themselves against the perceived achievements, or mothering ability, of others would demonstrate further that:

we are neither in the amphitheatre, nor on the stage, but in the panoptic machine, invested by its effects of power, which we bring to ourselves since we are part of its mechanism. (Foucault 1977, p. 217)

The rise and role of social media and celebrity culture was highlighted as a highly and ever expanding influential interpersonal aspect of modern motherhood. Facebook (2004) in particular was highlighted by participants (Kate, Louise and Gemma) as something that, '*can turn into a bit of a monster*' (Kate), adding to the pressure of modern motherhood. Awareness was demonstrated that social media does not reflect reality. Louise, for example, described an awareness of Facebook as '*the best bits and you don't see the rest of it*' however, despite this awareness, Louise also reflected on the way social media makes her '*worry and constantly thinks, is my child happy? well their child is always happy*'.

This echoes the exploration of online social networking earlier in this book (Chapter 3) and the normalisation in recent years of members of society sharing all aspects of their lives online particularly through social media (McDaniel et al. 2011; Anderson and Grace 2015; Valchanov et al. 2016; Wu Song and Paul 2016). In terms of interpersonal surveillance, this can be associated with the constant social comparison mothers make between themselves '*leaving many mothers feeling overwhelmed and inadequate, when they saw other mothers who apparently "do it all"*' (Valchanov 2016, p. 59). This feeling is exacerbated at a potentially isolated time in a new mother's life and the negative impact of it was reinforced by Gemma when she recalled her feelings that '*oh my god, people are living the best all the time*'.

Similarly, Schoppe-Sullivan et al. (2016) found associations between the use of Facebook (2004), mothering identity and depressive symptoms, within their research they suggested that:

mothers who were more prone to seeking external validation for their mothering identity and perfectionistic about parenting experienced increases in depressive symptoms indirectly via greater Facebook activity. (Schoppe-Sullivan et al. 2016, p. 276)

The association between Facebook use and maternal well-being can be linked to levels of surveillance and the panoptic machine which, in this case, extends into the homes of new mothers through engagement with social media. This is particularly pertinent during the transition to motherhood when sites like Facebook offer the possibility of '*connection and affirmation*' (Schoppe-Sullivan et al. 2016, p. 277) but increase the exposure to '*intensive mothering*' (Hays 1996; Douglas and Michaels 2005) where mothers are '*striving to meet nearly impossible domestic and parenting ideals*' (Schoppe-Sullivan et al. 2016, p. 277) to the detriment of their mental health and may go some way to explaining why Gemma reflected that '*I find that... getting away from Facebook sometimes,' that helps*'.

Added Pressure of Media/Celebrity

Three participants (Louise, Gemma and Ruth) highlight the added pressure of the media and celebrity as a factor within modern motherhood.

> I do think there is a tendency, you know, it is all picture perfect..... You know you see a lot of celebrities around having babies and it's almost been glorified a little bit and you know it is beautiful... it is lovely and I wouldn't change it for the world but... there is.... There is a hard side to it as well and you're knackered (Louise);
>
> You read 'OK' magazine and it's so and so having a baby and they look amazing and they've got makeup on and you know, the baby's just sleeping calmly in their hands and I know, actually the reality is..... you've just seen that picture of me when I'd just had a baby and I look like I've been dragged up.....(laughs) I look like I've died and been brought back up! 'M' always says 'you look like you've died and we've wheeled you in for a happy photo...! (Laughs) and I do...... I'm dead behind the eyes (Louise);
>
> I don't know.... it's originated from celebrities and that kind of thing that have got..... That are back into their size 6 jeans 2 weeks after having a baby. I don't know if that's part of it but you know, they've got personal trainers and chefs and nannies and all this sort of stuff but you're doing it, you know, on your own. Give yourself a break... you know, you have

to prioritise and your kids should be the most important things (cuddles baby) (Ruth);

Because when you're…. tired and you're emotional and all that sort of stuff and you don't think about things rationally and you do get, get swamped with images of people doing things perfectly and doing it different to you. And you feel as though you're doing something wrong… and you're not! (Ruth);

People do put pressures on themselves. Whether it's because of what they see, in the media or and they don't… take into account that these people have got full time nannies….. and you put pressure on yourself to be the same and it's not realistic and why would you want to be like that? You're supposed to enjoy being at home with your child and being in your pyjamas until 11 o'clock and playing and laying on the floor with them and all that sort of stuff. Not spending the time cleaning your house, kids are only gonna be babies once (kisses baby – 'aren't you?'). (Ruth)

Awareness of 'Parenting Industry'

When asked about why they think parenting is given so much attention these days, two participants (Ruth and Jenny) highlighted a link to the notion of a parenting industry.

I do think it's become an industry….. Especially the sort of…. Earth mother ways of raising kids, it is sort of like, cashing in on peoples beliefs and vulnerabilities, definitely… it's like a wedding industry (laugh!) it is… it's like selling, selling you the perfect way to raise a child and its… its funny (laughs) (Ruth);

I think there's a bit of a money spinner on it as well now… because people have jumped on the bandwagon and people know that with a parenting book, whatever it is, people are so desperate in those early weeks to get their baby to sleep you will buy every book that tells you 'we'll get your baby to sleep' … so I think that's part of it. (Jenny)

Henderson et al. (2015, p. 516) highlight how *'public discourses of motherhood'* can increase feelings of anxiety in mothers, even when they do not *'fully subscribe to the ideology'* (Henderson et al. 2015, p. 516).

Similarly, Beaupre Gillespie and Schwartz Temple (2011) recognised the resistance that some mothers demonstrate towards the dominant discourses as they reflected on how many times during their interviews they heard the phrase *'I'm not like the other mothers'* (Beaupre Gillespie and Schwartz Temple 2011, p. 44) and how despite an awareness and dislike of the dominant discourses and the *'emotional and isolating'* impact of motherhood ideologies, there is still an internalised impact from them, as demonstrated by Ruth and Jenny, who both displayed an awareness of the dominant discourses within modern motherhood, particularly in relation their awareness and concerns that parenting has become *'an industry… cashing in on peoples beliefs and vulnerabilities'* (Ruth).

This awareness also concurs with the suggestions put forward by Henderson et al. (2010) who recognised the power that interpersonal relationships, between mothers, have in reinforcing Foucault's panoptic machine through *'interpersonal communication and observation, ranging anywhere from conversations about children's appropriate developmental milestones to a covert, silent monitoring'* (Henderson et al. 2010, p. 231). Similarly, the rise in celebrity culture was highlighted as adding pressure to modern motherhood with Gemma, Ruth and Louise reporting unrealistic expectations and added pressure to be *'picture perfect'* (Louise) partly as a result of the presence of celebrity mothers in the media. Participants were aware however, when discussing both social media and celebrity culture, of the idealised nature of the images that are transmitted to them and the role that, combined with the notions of expert advice and rise in parenting education, can promote a culture of *'selling you the perfect way to raise a child'* (Ruth). Participants demonstrated an understanding of their role in the *'parenting industry'* (Guldberg 2009), but ultimately find it difficult not to internalise these ideologies and *'feel as though you're doing something wrong….. and you're not!'* (Ruth/P8/T5/I8). Douglas and Michaels (2005, p. 25) relate this tension to mothers feeling *'simultaneously guilt ridden and ready for an uprising'*.

Through a feminist post-structuralist lens, participants demonstrated that they were able to recognise their position within the parenting industry (Guldberg 2009), therefore challenging Foucault's (1977) belief that all members of society move through the panoptic machine unaware. The pressure in this instance relates more to the difficulty in challenging and resisting (Henderson et al. 2015) the ideology that is so deeply entrenched in modern motherhood.

Summary

This chapter has, through exploration of the key literature and extracts from the data collected within this research considered the different ways in which new mothers feel judged in modern parenting. Different forms of surveillance that are embedded into the everyday experiences of new mothers have been explored and the different reactions to them, considered.

References

Anderegg, D. (2003). *Worried All the Time: Over-Parenting in an Age of Anxiety and How to Stop It*. London: Free Press.

Anderson, W. K. Z., & Grace, K. E. (2015). 'Taking Mama Steps' Towards Authority, Alternatives, and Advocacy. *Feminist Media Studies, 16*(6), 942–959.

Beaupre Gillespie, B., & Schwartz Temple, H. (2011). *Good Enough Is the New Perfect*. Toronto, ON, Canada: Harlequin.

CANparent. (2012). *CANparent—Classes and Advice Network*. Available at http://www.parentinguk.org/canparent/network Accessed 13 January 2020.

Cunningham, H. (2012). *The Invention of Childhood*. London: BBC Books.

Currie, J. (2008). Conditions Affecting Perceived Coping for New Mothers, Analysis of a Pilot Study, Sydney, Australia. *International Journal of Mental Health Promotion, 10*(3), 34–41.

Czerniawski, G., & Lofthouse, R. (eds.). (2018). *Bera Bites Issue 1: Early Childhood*. London: British Education Research Association. Available at https://www.bera.ac.uk/publication/issue-1-early-childhood. Accessed 13 January 2020.

Davis, A. (2012). *Modern Motherhood: Women, Family and England 1945–2000*. Manchester: University Press.

Douglas, S. J., & Michaels, M. M. (2005). *The Mommy Myth: The Idealization of Motherhood and How It Has Undermined All Women*. New York: Free Press.

Dreyfus, H. L., & Rabinow, P. (1982). *Michael Foucault: Beyond Structuralism and Hermeneutics*. London: Harvester Wheatsheaf.

Facebook. (2004). Available at https://www.facebook.com/facebook. Accessed 13 January 2020.

Foucault, M. (1977). *Discipline and Punish: The Birth of the Prison*. London: Penguin.

Furedi, F. (2008). *Paranoid Parenting: Why Ignoring the Experts May Be Best for Your Child*. Wiltshire: Continuum.

Garrett, P. M. (2017). Wired: Early Intervention and the 'Neuromolecular' Gaze. *British Journal of Social Work, 0*, 1–19.

Gerhadt, S. (2004). *Why Love Matters*. London: Routledge.

Gopnik, A. (1999). *How Babies Think*. London: Pheonix.

Guldberg, H. (2009). *Reclaiming Childhood: Freedom and Play in an Age of Fear*. London: Routledge.

Hays, S. (1996). *The Cultural Contradictions of Motherhood*. London: Yale University Press.

Henderson, A., Harmon, S., & Houser, J. (2010). A New State of Surveillance: Applying Michael Foucault to Modern Motherhood. *Surveillance and Society, 7*(3/4), 231–247.

Henderson, A., Harmon, S., & Newman, H. (2015). The Price Mothers Pay, Even When They Are Not Buying It: Mental Health Consequences of Idealized Motherhood. *Sex Roles, 74*, 512–526.

Holloway, S., & Pimlott-Wilson, H. (2012). Any Advice Is Welcome Isn't It? Neoliberal Parenting Education, Local Mothering Cultures, and Social Class. *Environment and Planning, 46*, 94–111.

Kerrick, M., & Henry, R. L. (2017). 'Totally in Love': Evidence of a Master Narrative for How New Mothers Should Feel About Their Babies. *Sex Roles, 76*(1), 1–16.

Lee, E., Bristow, J., Faircloth, C., & Macvarish, J. (2014). *Parenting Culture Studies*. London: Palgrave Macmillan.

McDaniel, B. T., Coyne, S. M., & Holmes, E. K. (2011). New Mothers and Media Use: Associations Between Blogging, Social Networking and Maternal Well-Being. *Maternal Child Health, 16*(1), 1509–1517.

McNay, L. (1992). *Foucault and Feminism*. London: Polity Press.

Moss, P. (2017). Power and Resistance in Early Childhood Education: From Dominant Discourses to Democratic Experimentation. *De Gruyter Open, 8*(1), 11–32.

Musgrave, J. (2010). Educating the Future Educators: The Quest for Professionalism in Early Childhood Education. *Contemporary Issues in Early Childhood, 11*(4), 435–442.

Murray, J. (2018). In Praise of Early Childhood Educators. *International Journal of Early Years Education, 26*(1), 1–3.

National Health Service (NHS). (2017). *Health Benefits of Breastfeeding for Your Baby.* Available at http://www.nhs.uk/conditions/pregnancy-and-baby/pages/why-breastfeed.aspx. Accessed 13 January 2020.

Ramazanoglu, C. (1993). *Up Against Foucault: Explorations of Some Tensions Between Foucault and Feminism.* London: Routledge.

Rose, N. (1999). *Governing the Soul: The Shaping of the Private Self* (2nd ed.). London: Free Association Books.

Schoppe-Sullivan, A. J., Yavorsky, J. E., Bartholomew, M. K., Sullivan, J., Lee, M. A., Kamp Dush, C. M., et al. (2016). 'Doing Gender Online: New Mothers' Psychological Characteristics, Facebook Use, and Depressive Symptoms. *Sex Roles, 76,* 276–289.

Simonsardottir, S., & Gislason, I. V. (2018). When Breast Is Not Best: Opposing Discourses on Breastfeeding. *The Sociological Review, 61,* 1–7.

Solihull Approach Parenting. (2012). *Understanding Your Child.* Available at http://www.solihullapproachparenting.com/. Accessed 13 January 2020.

Valchanov, B. L., Parry, D. C., Glover, T. D., & Mulcahy, C. M. (2016). 'A Whole New World': Mothers Technologically Mediated Leisure. *Leisure Sciences, 38*(1), 50–67.

Vandenbroeck, M., De Vos, J., Fias, W., Mariett Olsson, L., Penn, H., Wastell, D., et al. (2017). *Constructions of Neuroscience in Early Childhood Education.* London: Routledge.

Wall, G. (2017). 'Love Build Brain': Representations of Attachment and Children's Brains in Parenting Education Material. *Sociology of Health & Illness, 2*(2), 1–15.

Wallbank, J. A. (2001). *Challenging Motherhood(s).* London: Prentice Hill.

Wastell, D., & White, S. (2017). *Blinded by Science: The Social Implications of Epigenetics and Neuroscience.* Bristol: Policy Press.

Winnicott, D. (1964). *The Child, the Family and the Outside World.* London: Penguin Books.

Wu Song, F., & Paul, N. (2016). Online Product Research as a Labor of Love: Motherhood and the Social Construction of the Baby Registry. *Information, Communication and Society, 19*(7), 892–906.

6

The Internalisation of 'Normalising Judgement': The 'Good Enough' Mother and Silences Within Modern Motherhood

Introduction

This chapter centres around Winnicott's (1964) perspective of the good enough approach and will be linked to current research and different perspectives regarding levels of surveillance within modern motherhood. This section will also consider intrapersonal surveillance as the most powerful level of surveillance. By considering interpersonal surveillance as a factor that will influence the experiences of motherhood, it is possible to reflect on the impact of it in regards to the internalisation of the normalising judgements that have been explored throughout this book and ultimately how this internalisation correlates to Foucault's (1977) concepts of 'the examination'; the final component of the instruments of correct training. Reflections from the survey and photo-elicitation interviews will focus on the 'all-Consuming' Pressure on Self to be 'Super-Mum'.

© The Author(s) 2020
H. Simmons, *Surveillance of Modern Motherhood*,
https://doi.org/10.1007/978-3-030-45363-3_6

The 'Good Enough Mother' Discourse

Within her research into maternal mental health, Currie (2008) relates the notion of being a 'good enough' mother to coping with the demands of the new role. Currie defines coping as including:

> efforts to manage stressful, challenging or difficult events, and is affected by lifestyle changes experienced since the birth of a child, the general difficulty of the mothering role and social pressures to succeed in that role. (Currie 2008, p. 34)

The research conducted by Currie (2008) provides essential insight into some of the factors that may increase motivation for attending parenting classes. She describes the link between being *'good enough'* and *'a sense of feeling in control'* (Currie 2008, p. 35), similarities can be made here to the work of Winnicott (1964) who also placed high emphasis on the importance of feeling 'good enough' as a mother.

This striving for feeling in control in a situation that can be very different from the daily realities of life before children could, according to Currie, encourage and empower mothers to seek to form strategies that can be implemented to go some way to restoring those feelings of control. In this respect, rather than being exposed to different forms of the *'parenting culture'* (Furedi 2008; Lee et al. 2014), attending a parenting course could be viewed as a proactive measure taken by new mothers to restore the feeling of control in their lives. The concern should perhaps be with the mothers who do not feel able to access the different forms of parenting support available to them. The stigma associated with admitting to somehow not be coping and the association with being 'good enough' put these women in a potentially vulnerable position (Currie 2008).

It is during the transition period into new motherhood that the feelings of coping or not coping are at their highest: *'a changed self-identity, reduced freedom and levels of tiredness never experienced before'* (Currie 2008, p. 36) are all factors contributing to these feelings. It is only when mothers take back some of the control by implementing strategies and building self-confidence that the stress and potential impact of that loss of control can be reduced. In this sense, parenting courses have the opportunity for mothers to reflect on their experiences and feel 'good enough'. Similarly, in their exploration of modern motherhood, Beaupre Gillespie and Schwartz Temple (2011, p. 5), relate the developing feelings of being in control to an acceptance of feeling 'good enough'. They suggest that generationally, more is expected of mothers than ever before and they relate this expectation to a feeling of responsibility within modern mothers in relation to the historical battles with equality. This manifests itself now as a feeling within modern motherhood that '*We are supposed to have it all*' Beaupre Gillespie and Schwartz Temple (2011, p. 4), including engaging fully with education and career pathways alongside being a devoted, natural and responsive mother. According to their research this sense of responsibility has led to an internalised feeling of pressure whereby '*perfection became an addiction, motherhood a competitive sport*' (Beaupre Gillespie and Schwartz Temple (2011, p. 4), only lessened when mothers relinquish the belief that '*you can do anything*' means '*you can do everything*' (Beaupre Gillespie and Schwartz Temple (2011, p. 4) and move forward within their own secure identity (Bassin et al. 1994; Miller 2005).

This tension is exacerbated when considered alongside other societal messages through developmental psychology *where 'mothers are portrayed as so central to, and absorbed within their children's development that any assertion of power or independence on their parts appears to be at the expense of damaging their children*' (Burman 2008, p. 134). With such conflicting discourses embedded into the psyche of society, it is little wonder that motherhood brings with it a deep challenge in relation to the navigating, resisting or reshaping of these discourses.

This feeling of taking back control of their lives can also be associated with the previously explored rise in online communities whereby parents use the forums, and advice available to them, to share experiences of the day to day aspects of being a new parent. The popularity of the online parenting website '*Mumsnet*' (Mumsnet 2000) provides opportunities for parents, usually mothers, to post questions and wait for helpful responses. Within their investigations of '*Mumsnet*' (Mumsnet 2000) as a new form of feminism, Pedersen and Smithson (2013, p. 100) describe motivations for accessing online communities as '*the need for support and advice*', in this respect then, although accessing online forums bring with it issues in relation to increased feelings of inadequacy (McDaniel et al. 2011; Valchanov et al. 2016) in relation to exposure to aggressive and judgemental responses to posts, the initial motivations for accessing advice comes from parents trying to create the strategies that they can implement in order to return the sense of control highlighted by Currie (2008).

The rise in the attention on parenting has also been linked to the increasingly popular makeover television programmes such as '*Supernanny*' (Channel 4, 2004–2012). With Furedi (2008) describing the rise in such advice forums as directly linked to the '*professionalisation of parenting*' (Furedi 2008, p. 180), whereby a:

> lack of belief in parental competence has been absorbed by contemporary culture and is regularly communicated to the public through sensational accounts about the failure of fathers and mothers. (Furedi 2008, p. 180)

During his collection of 23 interviews of first-time parents though, Gambles (2010, p. 707) found that mothers who have watched such programmes '*demonstrated resistance and scepticism of the techniques and approaches espoused by supernanny*'. It is interesting to consider how some mothers use makeover TV and other advice forums as a way of empowering their own situation and boosting their self-esteem and overall parenting skills (Gambles 2010), linking to both empowerment and autonomy. Other sources, however, question the motivation of such programmes. Lunt (2008) in his analysis of makeover TV remained unsure about the possible implications of such media and questioned whether similar programmes lead to '*docile subjects*' (Lunt 2008, p. 545) or indeed, whether opportunities to reflect on parenting '*pragmatically facilitates self-help in parents*' (Lunt 2008, p. 545). This dichotomy relates back to the earlier discussion surrounding the rise in influential social media and how it can promote practical support and source of community (Valchanov et al. 2016) in some cases and a source for reducing societal connectedness (McDaniel et al. 2011) in others. The tension between whether parenting education is an oppressive or an empowering tool appears to be at the very heart of this debate and is a theme running through each dominant discourse.

Johnson et al.'s (2009) research into breastfeeding practices also resonates with this theme and recognises the different ways mothers react to 'expert' advice. Johnson et al. (2009) and Currie (2008) both suggest that it is the very act of trying to take control back that leads women to search for strategies, such as those found within parenting courses, and how this perception of control can be linked to coping and being 'good enough'. Similarly, Thomson et al. (2011) in their research of modern motherhood and the vast amount of contradictory, and at times, judgemental advice from experts, discuss *how* mothers process the advice they are exposed to. Mothers, they suggest, develop the skill of becoming selective with regard to the many different forms of advice available to them. Thomson et al. (2011, p. 156) acknowledge though, that this requires some '*affective manoeuvring*'.

It is interesting to consider the various forms of advice as a potential empowering opportunity, at a time where there is more available information than ever before, if mothers are able to extract from it helpful information and not engage with concepts that they do not consider to be relevant to them or their baby. In this research it was essential to capture the experiences of mothers who have been 'exposed' to the parenting industry and listen to how they found ways to navigate this.

Research (Furedi 2008; Lee et al. 2014) has been explored that suggests that, through parenting education, mothers are manipulated, and insecurities heightened at an already potentially vulnerable and isolating time of their lives. Other perspectives though (Barlow and Coe 2012), suggested that universal parenting courses provide an opportunity for mothers to socialise with other mothers, reduce isolation encourage reflective parenting. Supporters of parenting courses would suggest that the different forms of advice be it baby manuals, makeover TV, website forums and in particular the increasingly popular parenting intervention programmes offer comfort and in fact, build confidence for new parents. The issue though, according to Furedi (2008, p. 183) is not '*whether parenting needs to be learned but whether it can be taught*' and how the rise in parenting education, as outlined within this chapter undermines the value of companionable learning (Roberts 2010) as a crucial component of the emergence of strong relationships.

Returning to the work of Foucault (1977), the desire that mothers feel to be 'good enough' comes not exclusively from the judgements made by those in positions of power, for example health visitors, midwives or from educational settings, but also from other mothers. As explored in Chapter 5, the pressure and feelings of judgement from the surveillance of other mothers may go some way to providing insight into the motivations of attending a parenting course. Rose (1999) agrees that the internalisation and scrutiny of motherhood creates a '*constant scrutiny of our inherently difficult interactions with our children and each other, a constant judgement of their consequences for health, adjustment, development, and intellect*' (Rose 1999, p. 213).

With comparisons being made between mothers relating to the reaching of developmental milestones, achievements in sleep training and behaviour management techniques, the pressure is certainly on for mothers to feel 'good enough'. Linking again to Foucault's (1977) exploration of Bentham's '*panopticon*' whereby through constant surveillance and the manipulation of members of society, eventually '*universal norms*' are created where '*the disciplines...hierarchize individuals in relation to one another and, if necessary, disqualify and invalidate*' (Foucault 1977, p. 222).

This is further supported by Henderson et al. (2010) and their suggestion that 'interpersonal surveillance' is the most powerful level of surveillance in motherhood. In their research Henderson et al. (2010) also noted that the comparison of parenting methods, parenting styles and practices is at its '*most common amongst middle and upper-middle class mothers*' (Henderson et al. 2010, p. 234), supporting the previously mentioned research of Edwards and Gillies (2011) and Holloway and Pimlott-Wilson (2012).

Correlating further to the work of Henderson et al. (2010), explorations of contested ideologies of motherhood (Johnston and Swanson 2006; Kerrick and Henry 2017) associate the internalisation of pressures with the transmission of messages throughout society. Johnston and Swanson (2006) refer to these messages as:

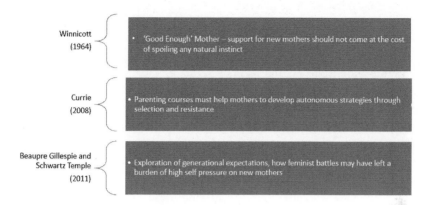

Winnicott (1964)
• 'Good Enough' Mother – support for new mothers should not come at the cost of spoiling any natural instinct

Currie (2008)
• Parenting courses must help mothers to develop autonomous strategies through selection and resistance

Beaupre Gillespie and Schwartz Temple (2011)
• Exploration of generational expectations, how feminist battles may have left a burden of high self pressure on new mothers

Fig. 6.1 Key literature within 'good enough mother' discourse

events, actions and images we create, and we consume packaged meanings that are perpetuated by societal groups to make sense of the seemingly random behaviours, beliefs, values and identifies that we claim and perform'. (Johnston and Swanson 2006, p. 509)

The key literature explored within this discourse is outlined in Fig. 6.1.

The Internalisation of 'Normalising Judgement'

Staying within the second objective of this research which was to consider the constructs and experiences of modern motherhood in relation to different levels of surveillance, theme 6 relates to the 'all-consuming' pressure on self to be 'super-mum' and can be explored within both interpersonal and self-surveillance. By considering inter-personal surveillance as a factor that will influence the experiences of motherhood, it is possible to reflect on the impact of it in regards to the internalisation of the normalising judgements that have been explored throughout this chapter and ultimately how this internalisation correlates to Foucault's (1977) concepts of '*the examination*'; the final component of the instruments of correct training, that through:

humble procedures of training and distribution. It operates through a combination of hierarchical observation and normalizing judgement. These combine into a central technique of disciplinary power: the examination. (Dreyfus and Rabinow 1982, p. 156)

Issues surrounding the internalisation of normalising judgement emerged predominantly during the late stages of the survey and interviews when mothers had reflected on how they felt in the early days of motherhood, considered advice and thought back to their experiences in attending a parenting course. The interviews took an almost chronological journey whereby once considering these early stages some of the wider social issues began to emerge surrounding interpersonal relationships and different types of surveillance that were felt by mothers as they try to build confidence and feel 'good enough'. What came to the fore next was participant reflections on their own positions within the discursive practices and how they reclaimed some of the control within the motherhood role and moved forward with confidence.

Theme 6: 'All-Consuming' Pressure on Self to Be 'Super-Mum'

This theme also provided evidence of self-surveillance with the internalisation of pressures to feel a certain way about motherhood, particularly in relation to bonding and attachment. As in theme 2, mothers demonstrated awareness of this form of surveillance and displayed a shift in confidence when reflecting on the end of the first year in the child's life when they perceived themselves as becoming the expert (Table 6.1).

Pressure on Self ('Mother's Guilt')

When asked the question 'do mothers put pressure on themselves' all seven interview participants (Clare, Jenny, Priya, Ruth, Gemma, Louise and Kate), agreed that they do.

Table 6.1 Issues within theme 6

- Pressure on self ('Mother's guilt')
- Feeling of taboo topics around motherhood (not all fairies and flowers)
- Going back to work
- Anger at partner for not 'doing it right'
- Frustration with other family members
- Concerns about post-natal depression
- Reclaiming control
- Learning to trust own instincts

You feel like a swan so you give off the air of being really confident and everything's going really smoothly and underneath you're sort of paddling as hard as you can to kind of keep things going (Kate);

I like to keep fit, I like to be a good wife, I like to provide food, I like all their clothes to be clean, I like the house to be tidy, I like to do really well at my job... but at some point..... you can't be all those people and be 100% of all those people and I know I put massive pressure on myself and that is only from me to blame (Kate);

Even the most confident of people.... I see that they probably felt very similar to how I did and I think .... that comes from the expectations of what it's gonna be like you know, the fact now that most girls that have babies have had careers they've worked and you know.... the reality is that I think it's the hardest thing you'll ever do.... So you know, you do put pressure on yourselves (Louise);

I think you probably (have an) internal battle that you're kind of fighting against (Gemma);

You can feel yourself doing it and I have to stop myself sometimes and say it doesn't matter if the house isn't perfect and if the carpet needs hoovering? If you're my friend and you're coming round to my house, then, you know, what does it matter? (Ruth);

You do, you just feel you have to do the right thing and be the best ....but its ok not to be (Priya);

There is some sort of weird, hormonal, emotional thing that just completely takes over and I always thought I was quite level headed and sort of black and white about things and this completely floored me (Jenny);

> I've often said, 'oh I'm not doing a very good job'....... 'I'm the worst
> mum in the world some days'... you know when you just can't get your
> head round things......I think talking to other people makes you realise
> you're not a bad mum.....it's just a learning curve. Its day by day and
> everyone, they're all different (Clare);
> You put so much pressure on yourself and that 'mothers guilt' that
> just..... I just never knew that something like that could exist! Or where
> it comes from, even when you're thinking about it really logically, it's just
> all-consuming isn't it? (Jenny)

Within the theme, all seven mothers give overwhelmingly similar answers
regarding internalised pressure which correlate with the idea of fighting
an *'internal battle'* (Gemma) and an *'all consuming'* (Jenny) sense of
'mothers guilt' (Jenny). Kate described feeling like *'a swan so you give
off the air of being really confident and everything's going really smoothly
and underneath you're sort of paddling as hard as you can to kind of keep
things going'* and Clare reporting experiences of *'I've often said, oh I'm not
doing a very good job..... I've sat and thought, oh I'm the worst mum in
the world some days'*. These findings relate to ideologies of motherhood
as something to be considered natural and instinctive (Wallbank 2001;
Douglas and Michaels 2005; Choi et al. 2005; Beaupre Gillespie and
Schwartz Temple 2011) and to research by Miller (2005) who suggests
that, during her research:

> women claim that they do not feel like mothers and can express concerns
> that they are fearful they will be 'found out'. Such worries are deeply
> rooted in perceptions of the moral context in which mothering occurs.
> (Miller 2005, p. 15)

From a feminist perspective, Miller (2005) also acknowledges the power
of self-surveillance and how this is intensified by the discursive practices so deeply entrenched within societal norms. In Foucauldian terms,
'the examination' (Foucault 1977, p. 184) has become the judgement
passed by mothers themselves in relation to their own ability. Here the
normalising techniques have served to *'define practices which fall outside
their system as deviant behaviour in need of normalization'* (Dreyfus and

Rabinow 1982, p. 198). As demonstrated from all interview participants, this internalisation can be associated with increased pressures
that mothers feel within modern society, creating this '*internal battle*'
(Gemma) due to higher expectations placed on them as a result of '*significant benefits from feminist campaigns.... For example, educational and
employment opportunities, a new ability to control their fertility and equality
legislation*' (Davis 2012, p. 212). These benefits, whilst extremely positive for women, do bring with them a heavy burden to access and achieve
within all of the available opportunities, further demonstrated by Kate
later on in the interviews who noted '*I like to keep fit, I like to be a good
wife, I like to provide food, I like all their clothes to be clean, I like the house
to be tidy, I like to do really well at my job*'.

Feeling of Taboo Topics Around Motherhood (Not All Fairies and Flowers)

Three participants (Gemma, Priya and Clare) made comments about
their experiences followed by questions referring to the seemingly taboo
topic they were referring to.

> I used to think, like when he was a baby 'oh, he's being really naughty'
> but he wasn't naughty, he was just being.... He was just there but perhaps
> because I wasn't in the right place I would just think 'it's just being ....
> Annoying'. That's really bad isn't it??? (Gemma);
> Some children just seem to do what their parents ask and you're like
> (pulls a face) 'Why doesn't mine? Just one time?'.... and then sometimes
> now he does, just say 'ok' and you're like 'ok!' I'm in control!!! It's bad
> that you feel like that isn't it? (Gemma);
> It's not all that great at the beginning. It's not all like fairies and you
> know.... You look at your baby lovingly.... It doesn't always work like
> that (Priya);
> Before I was like, as though, oh, you can't really say that, you're a
> mum, you're not allowed to say things like that... I feel as though .....
> it's not just all flowers and hearts. It's difficult, it's the hardest thing you'll
> ever do. It's the hardest thing I've ever done. (Clare)

Concerns expressed by mothers related to a feeling of certain aspects of motherhood being 'taboo' and how, if expressed, would suggest that they are either not coping or not responding to motherhood in the natural, instinctive way that is embedded into motherhood ideologies, internalised by society and which has the potential to undermine maternal well-being. Examples of these '*confessions of maternal shortcomings*' (Beaupre Gillespie and Schwartz Temple 2011, p. 58) came in the form of reflections from mothers on the difficulty and pressure to form an attachment with their babies immediately after birth including '*you can't really say that, you're a mum, you're not allowed to say things like that*' (Clare/P5/T6/I2). Both Priya and Clare discussed the pressure from society to '*feel this connection straight away*' (Priya). Priya reflected that '*it's not all that great at the beginning. It's not all like fairies and …. You look at your baby lovingly*', similarly, as noted by Clare, '*it's not just all flowers and hearts. It's difficult, it's the hardest thing you'll ever do*'.

Correlating with this, during the interviews themselves and afterwards as discussed within the methodology when reflecting on the challenges and my role as the researcher, a number of participants (Louise, Gemma and Clare) sought out reassurance from me regarding the nature of their responses, there was a feeling that they had in some way spoken out of turn. On two occasions during the interview Gemma stopped in mid-sentence and said '*that's really bad isn't it?*' and '*it's bad that you feel like that isn't it?*'. On both occasions Gemma was discussing her annoyance at her son's behaviour and once she had expressed her annoyance and subsequently questioned herself for it, she reflected that '*I've probably made him naughtier in a way, with the way I've dealt with that*'.

This can be associated with a transmitted '*sense of shame*' which Foucault (1977, p. 10) suggests '*is constantly growing; the psychologists and the minor civil servants of moral orthopaedics proliferate on the wound it leaves*'. Gemma's reflections regarding what she saw as a benefit of the parenting course that she attended, relate to a sense of internalising not only the behaviour of her son but also a subsequent period of self-blame in which time, the behaviour and possible reasons for it, are deflected onto herself through her confirmed belief that her children are mimicking her own behaviour. Burman (2008) attributes the way that

mothers internalise the behaviours of their children to the societal association, through the portrayal of developmental psychology, between the
actions of the mother and strong positive outcomes for the child. In this
way, mothers have absorbed the message that their '*needs must be assim-
ilated to those of their children for them to avoid censure as bad mother*'
(Burman 2008, p. 134).

These taboo topics can also be explored in relation to how whether
forced or self-imposed, silences reinforce the dominant discourses within
modern motherhood. The belief that certain aspects of motherhood
cannot be spoken about negatively, or in some case at all, serve to
strengthen the impact of motherhood ideologies. Símonardóttir and
Gíslason (2018, p. 13) in their exploration of the internalisation of
breastfeeding advice for new mothers suggest that silence is '*always meaningful as it is accompanied by social and political judgments about what is
acceptable and unacceptable*'.

As previously explored, Clare's reflections that the parenting course
encouraged her to realise that the behaviour of her sons was as a direct
result of her own behaviour echoes Rose's (1999, p. 133) discussion
about motherhood and the '*criteria of normality*'. This criterion serves
to '*provide the means of identifying abnormality and the rationale for intervention when reality and normality fail to coincide*' (Rose 1999, p. 133).
Miller (2005) expresses further concern about the internalisation of such
taboo topics and how:

> ironically, by silencing ourselves and only retrospectively voicing accounts
> of normal difficulties and uncertainties, we help to perpetuate and repro-
> duce the myth that mothering is instinctive and natural. (Miller 2005,
> p. 26)

Going Back to Work

Two participants (Kate and Jenny) referred to going back to work as an
important part of their early experiences of motherhood.

> The job that I was in at the time, they didn't put me under pressure
> but they kind said 'no one else is going to be doing this work…so the

longer you're off'.... Work was everything before M came along and I think when you make those decision..... You're probably maybe not in the frame of mind. Not that the world ends but you kind of feel that you've got a personal responsibility to people (Kate);

Going back to work helped with that, nursery and work really helped I think because then you're not just H's mum, you're back to work, you both got a bit more of an equal relationship. (Jenny)

Kate returned to work 6 weeks after her first child was born and reflected that '*Work was everything before... I think when you make those decision..... You're probably maybe not in the frame of mind*'. Jenny who had a longer maternity leave with her first child reported how her return to work signalled a return to her own identity and how '*you're not just H's mum, you're back to work, you've both got a bit more of an equal relationship*'. Both of these reflections echo the work of Miller (2005, p. 113) who recognises the return to work for some mothers, as an opportunity for '*a greater sense of control in a life with glimpses, and sometimes more, of a pre-baby self and life*'.

Anger at Partner for Not 'Doing It Right'

Jenny referred to a feeling of anger towards her partner for managing tasks in the early days of parenting in the same way that she would.

We put a lot of pressure on ourselves..... And on others.... I remember not letting M make bottles up. I couldn't let him do it without watching him for weeks and weeks and if he hadn't completely levelled off or if there was a couple of ml more water than it said on the pack I would just flip! 'Are you trying to kill him?? he's going to really upset his tummy and he might die!'....all logic goes out of the .... it was just absolutely crazy and I don't know where that came from.... emotions, hormones, whatever (Jenny);

Going back to the emotional stuff, attachment thing. I want to make all the decisions, and I know that's not right and we need to talk about things but I almost feel like I know better and I should have the final say on everything... that's been the biggest challenge I think, that knowing that..... you're a team and finding your rhythm.... (Jenny)

These findings suggest that the level of autonomy and control a mother has on her return to work correlates to how helpful that can be in redefining an identity within motherhood. Similarly, within the constructs of self-surveillance, participants also reflected on their frustrations with partners and other family members in relation to care and decision-making, this can be linked to a sense of needing to regain some control. It was also acknowledged that the need for being in control was a component of mothers putting immense pressure on themselves, including difficulty in sharing decision making with partners when there is a perception that '*I know better and I should have the final say on everything*' (Jenny). The process of navigating the early stages of motherhood corresponded to a feeling of regaining some level of control, this related to different and varied factors for participants including returning to work, developing a sense of knowing 'the right way' to look after their baby and also an increased confidence and trust in their own ability as a mother. This change signals some level of resistance to the concepts of being, and remaining a 'docile body' in Foucauldian terms, and instead, working towards developing agency and autonomy within the mother role. Whilst Henderson et al. (2010) levels of surveillance may be embedded into motherhood practice, the reactions to these levels are not identical or static.

Frustration with Other Family Members

Ruth discussed frustrations with other family members, particularly grandparents.

> I do think that it's important that discipline is a constant through parents, grandparents, things like that......other people should do their best to respect how they know we want him raised. So dealing with... that is quite difficult cos if he is with grandparents or aunts and uncles for a certain period of time and he has been allowed to get away with things he knows he shouldn't be allowed to get away with...., And it's then your job to pull it back into line and then you come across as being mean mum. (Ruth)

Concerns About Post-natal Depression

Four participants (Louise, Gemma, Clare and Jenny) identified post-natal depression as either something they had been diagnosed with or something they were concerned about.

I think from a mental health point of view…. I think I was a bit 'doo lally'….. looking back…. I wasn't really that normal. For quite a while, I'm not saying that there was something mega wrong but I think it affected me more than I thought it was going to and I think…. I obsessed over everything to do with them… but it's not healthy for you is it? So I think for me, that's why I found them (the parenting course) really useful because it gave me something else to think about ……to know that it was totally normal (Louise);

It's taken quite a long time and (pause) I don't know if I had post-natal depression or something with H but, he was quite quick at like walking and everyone would be like 'oh my, he's amazing' and I'd think 'no he's not, he's just annoying!' do you know what I mean? But now, I can kind of appreciate who he is but it's taken a long time (Gemma);

I was suffering from post-natal depression. So after the course, I'd got myself back onto antidepressants (Clare);

I know I spoke to my sister a bit about post-natal depression and whether I should go and speak to the doctor because I was like 'I don't feel right' but there's still something in me like 'I can't go to the doctors and say this, I'm just really tired and emotional and hormonal'…. like the way I spoke to M and the things he did that just made me fly off the handle……. I very nearly punched M in the face!…….I should have perhaps gone to the doctors….. it's just 'am I depressed or am I just tired and is this just how new mums feel and is this just normal?' and you've nothing to compare it to have you?

I think that's the bit, actually, that gets missed in those early stages. Apart from in your 6 week check when you see the doctor who literally just says 'how are you feeling?…. didn't really dig into anything… just wanted to tick the boxes and get me off the list. Nobody actually asked or said anything about post-natal depression or what's normal, what the signs are…. somebody looking out for you. (Jenny)

Worryingly, in association with the power of self-surveillance, these reflections show concerns about post-natal depression with Louise and Jenny both wondering whether it was '*normal*' to feel the emotions they did in those early days of motherhood or whether they were displaying signs of undiagnosed post-natal depression. The impact of the ideologies of motherhood and feelings that are created as a result of '*unattainable image of infinite patience and constant adoration*' (Douglas and Michaels 2005, p. 2) leads to a deeper, more worrying concern that post-natal depression may be present when these ideologies are not fully realised. With Public Health England (2020) stating that '*perinatal mental health problems affect between 10 to 20% of women during pregnancy and the first year after having a baby*' (Public Health England 2020) and cost the '*NHS and social services around £1.2 billion annually*' (Public Health England 2020) then some of the underlying pressures and the '*master-narrative*' (Kerrick and Henry 2017, p. 1) of motherhood needs to be considered in relation to the sort of support that mothers really need.

With the emphasis and use of neuroscientific research by policy makers (e.g. *Helping Parents to Parent Report*, Clarke et al. 2017) to underline the direct association between the parenting of young children and cognitive outcomes, parenting intervention programmes are highly likely to continue to develop further in the near future. It is essential therefore to provide a balanced perspective in relation to the potential for help and the potential for hindrance for mothers that are increasingly exposed and encouraged to attend these programmes.

From a feminist post-structuralist perspective, the aim of this research is not to 'blame' a particular aspect of society, but to acknowledge the realities of modern motherhood and to develop an understanding of the experiences of participants. As suggested by Símonardóttir and Gíslason (2018, p. 14), once the dominant discourses surrounding modern motherhood are identified, '*we are much better equipped to disrupt and untangle these constructions and power relations and critically engage with the normalizing discourses*'.

The above discussion outlines the power that the combined levels of surveillance and disciplinary technologies have on the practice of motherhood and go some way to explaining why participants have highlighted, throughout both the survey and the interviews, the critical importance of a trusted, truthful social network of other mothers to share experiences with. Interestingly, when asked to rank statements relating to the benefit of attending a parenting course, the statement that was ranked the highest was '*this class gave me opportunities to meet other parents*' with 73% of participants strongly agreeing. Once again, the importance of social interaction and a supportive network is highlighted as a need for new mothers. As Douglas and Michaels (2005, p. 250) highlighted, motherhood, at its most enjoyable is a '*collective experience*', further supported by Davis's (2012, p. 212) observations regarding how important the development of social networks is for mothers in order to take '*mutual pleasure in the delight that motherhood could bring, but also with the aim of alleviating some of the difficulties and inequities that they faced*'. Despite some negative experiences in terms of interaction and competition with other women, overwhelmingly, it is the interaction and the opportunity to meet other mothers that led them to attend a parenting course in the first place. From a feminist post-structuralist perspective, it is this proactive strategy that brings the opportunity for empowerment, whilst interpersonal surveillance is no doubt a hugely important aspect of being a new mother, there is agency within this experience and the reactions to this level of surveillance are by no means one dimensional.

Reclaiming Control

Two participants (Louise and Jenny) both discussed the return of a feeling of control during the first year of having their baby.

> I think by that point you're starting to work out a bit... a bit more decisive and thinking 'well, no that not going to work for me....and this is why...' I think otherwise I would have just been a nervous wreck during that whole process! (Louise);
>
> You know we're still not there but around 10-12months there was a bit of a change because I relaxed a bit about it H, I don't know if it's when they turn 1 or what but we seemed to relax about sleeps, food and what not. (Jenny)

Echoing reflections regarding the beginning of being able to ignore contradictory advice, Jenny and Louise reported a shift as their babies moved towards turning 1-year-old and a feeling of regaining control. Louise reflected that she became a '*bit more decisive*' and Jenny reported that by the time her baby reach 10–12 months old she '*relaxed a bit*'. Miller (2005, p. 112) labelled this change '*a return to normal: becoming the expert*' and recognised this as linked to the passage of time and experience where mothers can begin to return to their identities with newly emerging confidence in their mothering ability and shifts '*that occur around perceptions of expert, authoritative knowledge as control in a life felt to be regained*' (Miller 2005, p. 112). This is further reinforced through the research of Arnold-Baker (2019, p. 260) and her recognition that maternal identity is not a '*fixed entity*' but something that requires interaction between '*social, personal ad spiritual*' (Arnold-Baker 2019, p. 271) dimensions. It is the opportunity for self-reflection upon these developments that lead mothers towards an '*existential view of self*' (Arnold-Baker 2019, p. 272).

It is interesting to consider this identity shift from a feminist post-structuralist perspective as an acceptance that 'being good enough' is indeed, enough in relation to the different reactions to the levels of surveillance within motherhood experiences. Whilst participants reported positively about this increase in confidence however, the fact that this emerges so late in relation to the transition into motherhood could suggest either a normal rite of passage that all mothers must go through or as a missed opportunity that can be associated with the internalisation of self-surveillance and its subsequent effects.

Learning to Trust Own Instincts

Louise linked this feeling of control to learning to trust her own instincts again.

> Because there's just so many, people tell you so many different ways. Doctors that talk about it and these professionals that talk about it..........actually, one thing I have learnt to do a lot more than I did before is trust my instincts and know that I understand what he wants

and no, he's not going to like that cos he doesn't like x, y and z....... I would say I'm a lot better..... I had instincts but my instincts went.... My common sense went out the window when I first had him... I just didn't trust them at first, I was just like 'yeah, I'll try what you said cos you're obviously better at this cos you're a professional' but it's not true isn't it...... you don't believe it cos you've never done it, you've just never done it..... That first time....you're just like well, that's wrong, this is wrong, they're not doing this as they should do.... Well obviously somethings going wrong in that whole process that we've got to change. (Louise)

A secured identity as an individual (Winnicott 1964) and a rise in levels of coping (Currie 2008) is a constructive development. Participants did reflect however, on the limitations in support for new mothers, including the influx of information given from health professionals which is not individualised in any way and does not encourage mothers to recognise themselves as the potential expert and instead, breeds a culture of belief that '*I'll try what you said cos you're obviously better at this cos you're a professional*' (Louise). Whilst it is encouraging to see that participants were able to reflect back and see how their confidence and self-belief has developed over time, arguably, the damage has already been done in relation to the impact on the experience of the early days of motherhood and as Louise concluded '*obviously somethings going wrong in that whole process that we've got to change*'.

Summary

This chapter has, through exploration of the key literature and extracts from the data collected within this research considered the internalisation of the different forms of surveillance within modern motherhood. This includes responses to feeling judged and how this can create worrying 'silences' within modern motherhood.

References

Arnold-Baker, C. (2019). The Process of Becoming: Maternal Identity and the Transition to Motherhood. *Existential Analysis, 30*(2), 260–274.

Barlow, J., & Coe, C. (2012). *Family Action—Perinatal Support Project. Research Findings Report*. Warwick: Warwick Medical School.

Bassin, D., Honey, M., & Kaplan, M. M. (1994). *Representations of Motherhood*. New Haven: Yale University Press.

Beaupre Gillespie, B., & Schwartz Temple, H. (2011). *Good Enough Is the New Perfect*. Don Mills, ON, Canada: Harlequin.

Burman, E. (2008). *Deconstructing Developmental Psychology* (2nd ed.). London: Routledge.

Choi, P., Henshaw, C., Baker, S., & Tree, J. (2005). Supermum, Superwife, Supereverything: Performing Femininity in the Transition to Motherhood. *Journal of Reproductive and Infant Psychology, 23*(2), 167–180.

Clarke, B., Younas, F., & Project Team and Family Kids and Youth. (2017). *Helping Parents to Parent*. London: Social Mobility Commission.

Currie, J. (2008). Conditions Affecting Perceived Coping for New Mothers, Analysis of a Pilot Study, Sydney, Australia. *International Journal of Mental Health Promotion, 10*(3), 34–41.

Davis, A. (2012). *Modern Motherhood: Women, Family and England 1945–2000*. Manchester: University Press.

Douglas, S. J., & Michaels, M. M. (2005). *The Mommy Myth: The Idealization of Motherhood and How It Has Undermined All Women*. New York: Free Press.

Dreyfus, H. L., & Rabinow, P. (1982). *Michael Foucault: Beyond Structuralism and Hermeneutics*. London: Harvester Wheatsheaf.

Edwards, R., & Gillies, V. (2011). Clients or Consumers, Commonplace or Pioneers? Navigating the Contemporary Class Politics of Family, Parenting Skills and Education. *Ethics and Education, 6*(2), 141–154.

Foucault, M. (1977). *Discipline and Punish: The Birth of the Prison*. London: Penguin.

Furedi, F. (2008). *Paranoid Parenting: Why Ignoring the Experts May Be Best for Your Child*. Wiltshire: Continuum.

Gambles, R. (2010). Supernanny, Parenting and a Pedagogical State. *Citizenship Studies, 14*(6), 697–709.

Guldberg, H. (2009). *Reclaiming Childhood: Freedom and Play in an Age of Fear*. London: Routledge.

Henderson, A., Harmon, S., & Houser, J. (2010). A New State of Surveillance: Applying Michael Foucault to Modern Motherhood. *Surveillance and Society, 7*(3/4), 231–247.

Holloway, S., & Pimlott-Wilson, H. (2012). Any Advice Is Welcome Isn't It?' Neoliberal Parenting Education, Local Mothering Cultures, and Social Class. *Environment and Planning, 46,* 94–111.

Johnson, S., Williamson, I., Lyttle, S., & Leeming, D. (2009). Expressing Yourself: A Feminist Analysis of Talk Around Expressing Breast Milk. *Social Science and Medicine, 69,* 900–907.

Johnston, D. D., & Swanson, D. H. (2006). Constructing the 'Good Mother': The Experience of Mothering Ideologies by Work Status. *Sex Roles, 54,* 509–519.

Kerrick, M., & Henry, R. L. (2017). 'Totally in Love': Evidence of a Master Narrative for How New Mothers Should Feel About Their Babies. *Sex Roles, 76*(1), 1–16.

Lee, E., Bristow, J., Faircloth, C., & Macvarish, J. (2014). *Parenting Culture Studies*. London: Palgrave Macmillan.

Lunt, P. (2008). Little Angels: The Mediation of Parenting. *Journal of Media & Cultural Studies, 22*(4), 537–546.

McDaniel, B. T., Coyne, S. M., & Holmes, E. K. (2011). New Mothers and Media Use: Associations Between Blogging, Social Networking and Maternal Well-being. *Maternal Child Health, 16*(1), 1509–1517.

Miller, T. (2005). *Making Sense of Motherhood: A Narrative Approach*. Cambridge: University Press.

Mumsnet. (2000). *About Us*. Available at https://www.mumsnet.com/info/about-us. Accessed 13 January 2020.

Pedersen, S., & Smithson, J. (2013). Mother's with Attitude—How the Mumsnet Parenting Forum Offers Space for New Forms of Femininity to Emerge Online. *Women's Studies International Forum, 38,* 97–106.

Public Health England. (2020). *Perinatal Mental Health*. Available at https://www.gov.uk/government/publications/better-mental-health-jsna-toolkit/4-perinatal-mental-health. Accessed 13 January 2020.

Roberts, R. (2010). *Wellbeing from Birth*. London: Sage.

Rose, N. (1999). *Governing the Soul: The Shaping of the Private Self* (2nd ed.). London: Free Association Books.

Símonardóttir, S., & Gíslason, I. V. (2018). When Breast Is Not Best: Opposing Discourses on Breastfeeding. *The Sociological Review, 66*(3), 1–7.

Thomson, R., Kehily, M. J., Hadfield, L., & Sharpe, S. (2011). *Making Modern Mothers*. Bristol: The Policy Press.

Valchanov, B. L., Parry, D. C., Glover, T. D., & Mulcahy, C. M. (2016). 'A Whole New World': Mothers' Technologically Mediated Leisure. *Leisure Sciences, 38*(1), 50–67.

Wallbank, J. A. (2001). *Challenging Motherhood(s)*. London: Prentice Hill.

Winnicott, D. (1964). *The Child, the Family and the Outside World*. London: Penguin Books.

7

Listening to Mothers: Reflections on Motherhood and Support for New Mothers

Introduction

This chapter will include insight into the participant views on the support currently offered to new mothers alongside an exploration of the current initiatives and strategies for new mothers. The third objective of this research was to produce a greater understanding of some of the pressures within modern motherhood in the UK today. The final theme that emerged from the findings related to 'reflecting on motherhood' whereby participants were asked to consider the most rewarding and challenging aspects of motherhood and also to reflect on how they believe new mothers could be best supported in the future. Extracts from the survey and photo-elicitation interviews will centre around reflections on the transition to motherhood.

Reflecting on Motherhood

The third objective of this research was to produce a greater understanding of some of the pressures within modern motherhood in the

© The Author(s) 2020
H. Simmons, *Surveillance of Modern Motherhood*,
https://doi.org/10.1007/978-3-030-45363-3_7

Table 7.1 Issues within theme 7

- Less stressful after having second child
- Most rewarding aspects of motherhood
- Most challenging aspects of motherhood
- Ideas about how mothers can be best supported

UK today. The final theme that emerged from the findings related to 'reflecting on motherhood'.

Theme 7: Reflecting on Motherhood

Reflections are presented within this theme with a focus on aspects of motherhood that individual participants found the most rewarding, challenging and opinions on how new mothers can be best supported (Table 7.1).

Less Stressful After Having Second Child

Three participants (Gemma, Ruth and Priya) discussed the more relaxed experience they had with their second child.

> Then second time it's a breeze! And you think 'how was it hard??' You're in that life, that situation, know what to expect (Gemma);
> But this time I'm more content and I actually….it's actually quite nice to have a bit of time at home. (Ruth);
> It's a shame really that you can't…… you don't feel the second, that you didn't feel with your first like you did with your second (Gemma);
> Just society… other mothers… everything. Everything together makes you feel like oh, you should be doing this at this stage, but. So yeah, I think we put a lot of pressure on ourselves but I really think that it's when you have your first child that you do it a lot more, when you've moved on from your first, you're like, 'ok its fine…..'. (Priya)

Most Rewarding Aspects of Motherhood

The participants all reflected on different aspects of motherhood as the most rewarding including breastfeeding (Kate), watching their children reach developmental milestones (Ruth, Priya, Clare and Jenny) and feeling more comfortable in the mother role (Gemma and Louise).

I think the fact that I could breastfeed her really really easily...... I'm really, really proud of that. And..... It's been rewarding that I've been able to have my own life in terms of work and from a just purely motherly point of view, and the fact that I've been able to feed them.... And I know that some people don't get that opportunity and it's not a judgement on them but it's just a personal thing (Kate);

I think, finally feeling comfortable and enjoying it a bit more (Gemma);

Oh, it is really rewarding! Just, each milestone that they reach like, when they first talk, when they crawl, when they go to walk.... when they go to school and they can first read. Everything is rewarding.....but can't imagine your life without them after (Priya);

Oh, I just, I wouldn't be without them. I mean, some days I could just scream but I wouldn't be without them. I.....we were trying for 3 and a half years before we had Z.... It's just like, seeing them grow and their personalities coming out, I mean they're both so funny... I wouldn't say I wouldn't have them, cos I love them to bits and they're definitely the most rewarding job I've ever done, if you think of it as a job (Clare);

Just seeing H grow up and change and learn new things and yeah I think that's it.... Everyday there is something that is rewarding, or that every day he makes me laugh. I never used to laugh every day. There was never anything that happened every day that was particular funny.... but there's always something funny that happens with H. So yeah, I thinks it's just watching him grow and change and learn new things. (Jenny)

On reflecting on the most rewarding aspects of motherhood, aside from finding joy from the children themselves as they grow and develop, and in observing 'each milestone they reach' (Priya), participants also reported a sense of achievement in relation to the personal aspects of motherhood such as being able to breastfeed, returning to work and feeling proud of their role in nurturing their children, echoing Winnicott's (1964) philosophy of the importance of enjoyment and self-identity. Louise and Gemma both reflected on the rewarding aspect of mothering coming from being able to find enjoyment and feeling more comfortable in the role, this correlates to the work of Zimmer-Gembeck et al. (2015) who found a direct link between efficacy, confidence and autonomy to levels of enjoyment and competence in motherhood.

Most Challenging Aspects of Motherhood

The participants all reflected on different aspects of motherhood as the most challenging including being decisive as a new parent (Louise, Jenny and Ruth), juggling many different responsibilities (Kate), the behaviour of the child (Gemma), breastfeeding (Priya) and post-natal depression and bonding (Clare).

> I would say it's that… the constant reassessing….'right then, this is where we are then….what are we gonna do from here….?' I think it just never expected the, the huge difference that it would have on your life so that was probably the most difficult thing…. The dawning… which is weird because you knew it would happen (Louise);
>
> You (used to) see people disciplining for one thing and then not another and you always think 'oh, I'll never do that….. I'll be really consistent' and then when you've got your own you know that they've got their own way of doing things or if they've had a bad day the day before or if they're teething or poorly. …. it's all so straight down the line isn't it when you've not got one and when you have… (Jenny);
>
> I think sticking to your own beliefs and the way that you want to do it when there are so many people (points to kitchen where husband is) telling you that you should be doing it a different way. Or…. interfering in how you want to do it. Letting things slide when they know that you wouldn't want them to slide…..if he's in the care of someone else (Ruth);
>
> The challenges are challenges that I've kind of put out their myself like the whole, wanting to be 'super-mum', wanting to be there to collect the kids every single day….. it's just kind of juggling it all the time and I think that's probably one of the hardest things… and I don't think that'll ever end because even though they'll be going to school, that'll be a whole new set of things to juggle (Kate);

Having a child that does not listen???? But then again, I think that's probably my way. I guess it is the way you do things that makes them no.... I don't know, I just think H is quite spirited and .... Wilful so it's, its difficult (Gemma);

I've always had depression, even before I had children, so I knew it was sort of gonna happen..... and me, getting my head around, it's not the kids cos ... when I had Z, I literally thought that he was crying just to annoy me so that was really difficult .... I think I was annoyed with myself because you hear some people say 'oh you get this overwhelming love when you first see them' and I didn't have that, it took us a while to bond and I think that admitting that's quite difficult, and admitting it in front of other mums is quite difficult... and I think that people should be more open..... it's not always instant and you don't always get that overwhelming love......it's like when you first meet someone, it's getting to know them... you've got a new person in your life and you've got to adapt to how they are and so, yeah it's, it's not easy. (Clare)

When considering the most challenging aspect of motherhood, participants reinforced the previous reflections from the early days of motherhood. Tiredness and lack of sleep was highlighted again here, however, some different responses were also given which show the unique experience of the participants themselves. Whilst Kate recognised the pressure she had placed upon herself to '*be super-mum*', Louise focussed more on the life changing experience motherhood is and how she '*never expected the huge difference it would have on my life*'. Other participants identified different aspects of motherhood to be the most challenging, Priya identified breastfeeding as her biggest challenge and Ruth identified '*sticking to your own beliefs and the way that you want to do it when there are so many people....... telling you that you should be doing it a different way*'.

Participants selected a different aspect as most challenging to them as an individual. Clare for example reflected on her experiences with post-natal depression that were discussed earlier in the chapter. Clare reported her biggest challenge as '*admitting*' she was struggling and taking the time to realise that, as with all other relationships in life, '*it's getting to know them and getting to like what they like*'. Although unique aspects of motherhood were expressed as the most challenging by participants, each participant's reflections relate to characteristics that can be associated with self-surveillance. Each mother related to a facet of their own behaviour, further strengthening the idea of self-surveillance as linked to an overriding societal '*bio-power*' (Dreyfus and Rabinow 1982, p. 143). Similarly, Rose (1999) in his exploration of the '*genealogy of modern self*' and the role that psychology as a domain of knowledge has played in the importance placed onto parenting education, stresses the pressure now placed on new mothers to '*precede the teacher*' and how:

> If she plays her part well, the child's future life chances will be immeasurably enhanced, if she fails through ignorance or impatience to realize or to actualize such a learning scheme, woe betide her child when he or she enters school. (Rose 1999, p. 182)

Overwhelmingly, the reflections of participants in relation to how they can be best supported suggest that mothers do not feel they need to be told how to look after their baby and they do not express desire to develop knowledge or insight into the neuroscientific development of their babies (Rose 1999; Burman 2008). Instead, they desire safe, informal, non-judgemental places to meet other people with children of a similar age and a chance to share experiences and feel valued as an individual human being. This resonates back to the work of Winnicott (1964) who outlined the importance of mothers finding their confidence through the affirmation of their own identity first. Winnicott suggested that through the developing recognition of the mother as a person separate from their child, the feeling of intense pressure can be reduced and a sense of enjoyment increased.

Bassin et al. (1994) recognise Winnicott's concepts and constructs of motherhood as '*being in some way even more difficult, and perhaps in some ways easier – at least more gratifying – than Winnicott imagined*' (Bassin et al. 1994, p. 160) but also saw the potential for Winnicott's philosophy had potentially positive implications for mothers and that '*allowing the mother to be a person first is the key to maternal resilience*' (Bassin et al. 1994, p. 160). Similarly, society has, since the post-1930s focus on motherhood (Humphries and Gordon 1993; Burman 2008; Cunningham 2012; Davis 2012) has served to add to the pressures on mothers through multiple layers of surveillance which reinforce the message that '*it is the duty of women to produce strong, obedient citizens upon whom the future strength and stability of the nation depends'* (Humphries and Gordon 1993, p. 49). Whilst participants displayed some difficulty in resisting this discourse, they did demonstrate an awareness of it and the way these societal messages lead to the internalisation of *'mother's guilt'*. Participants also demonstrated a clear recognition that more thought needs to put into the support currently available to new mothers.

Ideas About How Mothers Can Be Best Supported

The interview participants all reflected on different ways in which mothers can be best supported in the early days of motherhood including informal and localised support groups (Kate, Gemma, Clare), more early information regarding support groups (Louise) and neutral, individualised advice from health professionals regarding sensitive areas such as breastfeeding and the reaching of developmental milestone (Kate, Ruth, Priya and Jenny).

> People to not put pressure on them, particularly, say midwives and health care practitioners .....Because we all do feel like we're being judged and that's the worst feeling that you can have. So I think, anything that's in an informal setting where people can feel comfortable and confident to ask any questions that they might have.... I think anything too structured; people just feel pressures to... perform in a particular way rather than actually admitting where they are with things (Kate);
>
> Ideally, family. The family would be better, but we, we seem to have; we don't have that round here. Everybody's got their own lives, everybody's busy. But I think these Children's Centres are fantastic and the health visitors and the midwives, they're brilliant.... I think, my health visitor because she was so on the ball.... that was really good. But, you know, she was a mum herself so I think, you know, that she understood...... it's quite sad to know that some of them are closing down and I think that'll be a big loss.....I was just sat in the house, dreading going out and now I just get on with it but if it wasn't for the initial support from the Children's Centre, I wouldn't be where I am today. So yeah, I think more support for new mums from places like that is great (Clare);

Maybe a proactive you know, call, from the hospital? Or somebody to say … 'who have you actually made contact with? Or what groups are you getting out to?'……. in the first few weeks or the first month (Louise);

I think they need to have more options available to them, without the thought of being judged about which option they pick. So if you take breastfeeding and bottle feeding. For example, there should be just as much information about bottle feeding, sterilising, that kind of thing, as there is about breastfeeding, without the thought of 'I'm gonna be judged if I don't pick to do breastfeeding'….. there's all sorts of comparisons where certain things are pushed above another, you know, you should have this kind of pram, and you should have, this kind of bedding and this is the best mattress and the best cot and you should……. They're all the most expensive ones and you know, they all cost a fortune and it's not realistic for people to do that…. …. The entire system needs streamlining…. There's just so many different places that you can go to now…it's difficult to wheedle out what's right and what's wrong (Ruth);

Not having as much pressure from health visitors about what your child's doing. You know, saying they should be able to do this, that and the other at this age ….. I think just to be a bit more supportive rather than judgemental…….. It just makes you not want to call them or not want to go…..I'm sure people are like that… and then they just sit at home and cry about it instead. Just deal with it themselves…. having someone to talk to and you know, give advice but just that forcefulness needs to just go (Priya);

Just general, like, getting through the day! So it wasn't anything kind of specific. I don't know, I can't quite put my finger on it. I think what they need help with is being confident in their decisions, and not being compared to or told they should be doing things… or baby should be doing… x y and z by now….. They are all just so different (Jenny);

My health visitors were quite good. They weren't judgemental. I think the difficulty is you see so many health visitors, you haven't got that one person that knows your story or your situation …. When people were coming to the house in the really early day, that they were just ticking boxes, like they'd just got to get certain things checked off.

I remember there was one thing…. The health visitor rang me and I didn't answer my phone…. and I didn't call them back and then someone popped round and I didn't answer the door and then that was it, I was kind of forgotten about. And then a few weeks later when I went to get him weighed, somebody mentioned it, they said, 'oh yes I can see on the system that we've tried to call you and you didn't answer and popped round but there was no answer' and it was fine cos I was ok..... I was talking to mum about it and she was like 'what if you'd have been a really vulnerable mum? Surely you don't just knock on the door and then go away...?' So I think new mums... they do need a bit of persistence with the help, because you don't always want to go and tell people that you're not coping. (Jenny)

The role of the health professional has been continuously highlighted as important and when considering other forms of support, all participants outlined the significance of local support and the importance of having supportive, empathetic, *'proactive'* (Louise) health professionals. The overriding importance of not feeling judged by health professional was emphasised by all participants. As stated by Kate *'we all do feel like we're being judged and that's the worst feeling that you can have'* and therefore, informal support in the form of a setting where mothers *'feel comfortable and confident to ask any questions that they might have'* (Kate). Despite their experiences of attending a parenting course, participants recognised that with anything too structured or formalised, *'people just feel pressures to... perform in a particular way rather than actually admitting where they are with thing'* (Kate) and that new mothers need someone to *'talk to and you know, give advice but just that forcefulness needs to just go'* (Priya). The positive influence that her local Sure Start Children's Centre support gave her was reflected upon by Clare, who emphasised that *'if it wasn't for them I wouldn't be out and about in the first place doing what I'm doing now...I was just sat in the house, dreading going out and now I just get on with it'*.

Opportunities for mothers to self-reflect (Arnold-Baker 2019) and share experiences in a safe and non-judgemental environment, whilst being supported to enjoy these experiences with their own identity secured, has to be acknowledged as fundamental for new mothers. If the well-being and maternal resilience of mothers is secured then, as linking back to Winnicott's (1964) philosophy then the relationship and experiences of new mothers can be facilitated to be a positive, 'good enough' one.

The Voice of the Mother

As demonstrated throughout the exploration of the dominant discourses and themes throughout this book and within the underpinning conceptual framework (Fig. 7.1) there are several highly conflicting strands. These strands have been considered through a feminist post-structuralist worldview in order to explore modern motherhood, particularly in relation to different forms of surveillance that are embedded within these experiences.

What was clearly missing through the dominant discourses is the voice of the mother. With acceptance throughout the literature that 'parenting education' is indeed aimed at mothers, the varied experiences and reflections of mothers who have attended these courses are noticeably absent. As evidenced throughout this book, a purely post-structuralist perspective would not allow the research to acknowledge the opportunities for women to demonstrate agency or individualism within their experiences, whereas a purely feminist perspective would not provide opportunities for a deeper exploration of the wider social constructs that lie within the discursive practices of the participants. A combined feminist post-structuralist perspective therefore, as highlighted by Baxter (2003, p. 2) allowed the research to develop and explore the rich stream of evidence within the varied reflections of mothers and to acknowledge all possible experiences within the '*productive contradiction*' of the combined approach.

Summary

The findings of this research confirm that structural, interpersonal and self-surveillance (Henderson et al. 2010) are indeed embedded into our society and into the discursive practices within modern motherhood in the the UK today. Unlike Henderson et al. (2010) though, who found interpersonal surveillance to be the most powerful, this research recognises self-surveillance; the internalisation of the '*master narratives*'

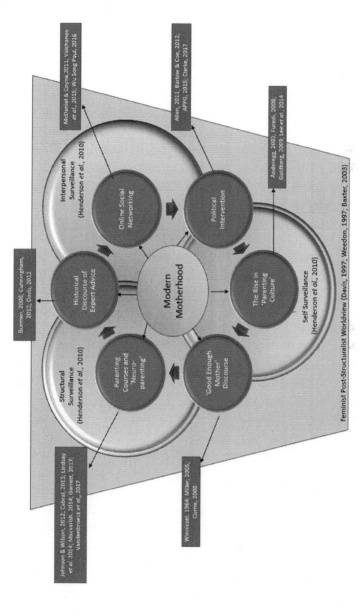

Fig. 7.1 Surveillance of modern motherhood: the conceptual framework

(Kerrick and Henry 2017, p. 1) as the most powerful level of surveillance. What is also clear from this research is that, by listening to the real experiences of mothers through a feminist post-structuralist lens, without the assumptions that mothers are simply '*docile*' (Foucault 1977, p. 136) victims of surveillance, the reactions to these levels can certainly demonstrate agency and autonomy. It is acknowledged, and will be considered further in the following chapter, that it is difficult to resist the dominant discourses, but through the development of individualised support systems that centre on informal, neutral and practical support for new mothers, along with opportunities for mothers to foster trusting and open social networks, mothers will feel empowered to share their experiences with honesty and move forward in the resisting and reshaping of the dominant discourses.

Research Conceptual Framework

A conceptual framework (Fig. 7.1) is presented which is shaped around the dominant discourses and themes embedded within the chapters of this book. Through a Feminist Post-Structuralist worldview, Henderson et al.'s (2010) levels of surveillance are provided (yellow circles) as embedded and experienced within the 6 dominant discourses and themes (blue circles) that emerged from the literature. These dominant discourses outline and highlight the different pressure points within modern motherhood stemming from historical interest and expert advice to more recently intensified pressures in the form of intrusion through social media platforms and government intervention programmes, all of which have served to heighten the opportunity for added pressure and attention on mothers. At the centre of these discourses is modern motherhood (green circle) and, in keeping with the feminist post-structuralist philosophical approach, the recognition that mothers have multiple and varied reactions to their experiences.

References

Allen, G. (2011). *Early Intervention: The Next Steps, an Independent Report to Her Majesty's Government by Graham Allen MP*. London: The Stationary Office.

All Party Parliamentary Group (APPG). (2015). *Conception to Age 2: First 1001 Days. Perinatal Inquiry—Evidence Sessions on First 1001 Days*. UK.

Anderegg, D. (2003). *Worried All the Time: Over-Parenting in an Age of Anxiety and How to Stop It*. London: Free Press.

Arnold-Baker, C. (2019). The Process of Becoming: Maternal Identity and the Transition to Motherhood. *Existential Analysis, 30*(2), 260–274.

Barlow, J., & Coe, C. (2012). *Family Action—Perinatal Support Project. Research Findings Report*. Warwick: Warwick Medical School.

Bassin, D., Honey, M., & Kaplan, M. M. (1994). *Representations of Motherhood*. New Haven: Yale University Press.

Baxter, J. (2003). *Positioning Gender in Discourse: A Feminist Methodology*. Hampshire: Palgrave Macmillan.

Burman, E. (2008). *Deconstructing Developmental Psychology* (2nd ed.). London: Routledge.

Cabral, J. (2013). The Value of Evaluating Parenting Groups: A New Researcher's Perspective on Methods and Results. *Community Practitioner, 86*(6), 30–33.

Clarke, B., Younas, F., & Project Team and Family Kids and Youth. (2017). *Helping Parents to Parent*. London: Social Mobility Commission.

Cunningham, H. (2012). *The Invention of Childhood*. London: BBC Books.

Currie, J. (2012). Conditions Affecting Perceived Coping for New Mothers: Analysis of a Pilot Study, Sydney, Australia. *International Journal of Mental Health Promotion, 10*(3), 34–41.

Davis, B. (1997). The Subject of Post-Structuralism: A Reply to Alison Jones. *Gender and Education, 9*(3), 271–283.

Davis, A. (2012). *Modern Motherhood: Women, Family and England 1945–2000*. Manchester: University Press.

Dreyfus, H. L., & Rabinow, P. (1982). *Michael Foucault: Beyond Structuralism and Hermeneutics*. London: Harvester Wheatsheaf.

Foucault, M. (1977). *Discipline and Punish: The Birth of the Prison*. London: Penguin.

Furedi, F. (2008). *Paranoid Parenting: Why Ignoring the Experts May be Best for Your Child*. Wiltshire: Continuum.

Garrett, P. M. (2017). Wired: Early Intervention and the 'Neuromolecular Gaze'. *British Journal of Social Work*, 1–19.

Guldberg, H. (2009). *Reclaiming Childhood: Freedom and Play in an Age of Fear*. London: Routledge.

Henderson, A., Harmon, S., & Houser, J. (2010). A New State of Surveillance: Applying Michael Foucault to Modern Motherhood. *Surveillance and Society, 7*(3–4), 231–247.

Humphries, S., & Gordon, P. (1993). *A Labour of Love: The Experiences of Parenthood in Britain 1900–1950*. London: Sidgwick and Jackson.

Johnson, R., & Wilson, H. (2012). 'Parents' Evaluation of 'Understanding Your Child's Behaviour', a Parenting Group Based on the Solihull Approach'. *Community Practitioner, 85*(5), 29–33.

Kerrick, M., & Henry, R. L. (2017). 'Totally in Love': Evidence of a Master Narrative for How New Mothers Should Feel About Their Babies. *Sex Roles, 76*(1), 1–16.

Lee, E., Bristow, J. Faircloth, C., & Macvarish, J. (2014). *Parenting Culture Studies*. London: Palgrave Macmillan.

Lindsay, G., Cullen, M., Cullen, S., Totsika, V., Bakopoulou, I., Goodlad, S., … Mantovani, I. (2014). *CANparent Trial Evaluation: Final Report, Research Report*. DfE: RR357.

McDaniel, B. T., Coyne, S. M., & Holmes, E. K. (2011). New Mothers and Media Use: Associations Between Blogging, Social Networking and Maternal Well-Being. *Maternal Child Health, 16*(1), 1509–1517.

Miller, T. (2005). *Making Sense of Motherhood: A Narrative Approach*. Cambridge: University Press.

Rose, N. (1999). *Governing the Soul: The Shaping of the Private Self* (2nd ed.). London: Free Association Books.

Song, F. W., & Paul, N. (2015). Online Product Research as a Labor of Love: Motherhood and the Social Construction of the Baby Registry. *Information, Communication & Society, 19*(7), 892–906.

Valchanov, B. L., Parry, D. C., Glover, T. D., & Mulcahy, C. M. (2016). 'A Whole New World': Mothers' Technologically Mediated Leisure. *Leisure Sciences, 38*(1), 50–67.

Vandenbroek, M., De Vos, J., Fias, W., Mariett Olsson, L., Penn, H., Wastell, D., & White, S. (2017). *Constructions of Neuroscience in Early Childhood Education*. London: Routledge.

Weedon, C. (1997). *Feminist Practice and Poststructuralist Theory: Second Edition*. Oxford: Blackwell Publishers.

Winnicott, D. (1964). *The Child, the Family and the Outside World*. London: Penguin Books.

Zimmer-Gembeck, M. J., Webb, H. J., Thomas, R., & Klag, S. (2015). A New Measure of Toddler Parenting Practices and Associations with Attachment and Mothers' Sensitivity, Competence, and Enjoyment of Parenting. *Early Child Development and Care, 185*(9), 1422–1436.

8

Conclusions and Implications for Policy, Research and Practice

Introduction

Within this chapter, key findings will be explored along with recommendations and reflections for future research, policy and practice.

Conclusion and Summary

Through an exploration of the first two emerging themes (T1—Navigating the early days of motherhood and T2—'Expert' advice and support for new mothers) within the findings there is a recognised feeling of shock, being unprepared and overwhelmed in the early stages of motherhood, linking back to the ideologies of motherhood as something that should be natural and instinctive (Choi et al. 2005; Douglas and Michaels 2005; Beaupre Gillespie and Schwartz Temple 2011). Recommendations can be made for some acknowledgement that the aforementioned feelings are not uncommon, and that confidence is something that develops over time with experience and appropriate support for new mothers (Winnicott 1964). This is supported by reflections from the participants who reported the developing ability to filter

© The Author(s) 2020
H. Simmons, *Surveillance of Modern Motherhood*,
https://doi.org/10.1007/978-3-030-45363-3_8

un-welcome or conflicting advice from baby manuals, popular parenting websites and from family, friends and health professionals, after a period of time, as confidence developed.

Through a feminist post-structuralist perspective these findings can be seen through the lens of multiple possibilities within the experiences of mothers including feeling dependent on and judged by others (Foucault 1977; Rose 1999) and finding agency and empowerment (Weedon 1997; Davis 1997; Baxter 2003), with time being the important variable to be recognised as an opportunity for confidence to grow alongside a regained feeling of coping (Currie 2008). Exploring the experiences of motherhood within a feminist post-structuralist perspective offers through post-structuralism; *a useful, productive framework for understanding the mechanisms of power in our society and the possibilities of change* (Weedon 1997, p. 10) whilst also acknowledging, through feminism, the importance of autonomy and resistance to the dominant discourses in a society where *to be inconsistent is to be unstable* (Weedon 1997, p. 10).

Consideration of theme 3 (T3—Reasons identified for going to a parenting course) and theme 4 (T4—Experiences of attending a parenting course) from the findings focussed on reflections of the parenting courses themselves and showed that the opportunity for building a social network and reducing the potential for isolation, were the main motivating factors in attending a parenting course. The evidence from within the findings also showed a desire for helpful and practical advice on aspects of parenting including sleep, breastfeeding and weaning. This challenges the government focus on parenting intervention programmes that offer psychoanalytical or neurodevelopmental programmes focussed on parenting style, childhood behaviour and an in-depth insight into child development (Johnson and Wilson 2012; Clarke et al. 2017). Reflections from the parenting course themselves showed that the importance of the role of the practitioner was crucial here. Participants responded negatively when they felt that health and early years practitioners had a hidden agenda including, 'pushing' them into breastfeeding or judging them if they were not able to or decided not to. Similarly, the importance of supportive relationships with other mothers during the parenting course was highlighted and acknowledgement given to competitive mothers having a negative influence on the experience of attending the parenting course, this important 'interpersonal relationship' supports the previously explored research by Henderson et al. (2010). Overall, the completion of the course itself leads to a sense of achievement and increased feelings of confidence and competence within participants. It can be acknowledged through this research that there is a place for parenting courses as a way to support mothers but it is important that they come from a practical, supportive and neutral position rather than grounded in neuroscientific and theoretical underpinnings, which have not been considered as useful for participants and indeed, seem to promote internalised feelings of judgement and added pressure.

Theme 5 (feeling judged) explored issues such as mothers feeling unable to make a doctor's appointment through the impression that they are being overly anxious or 'wasting the time' of doctors. Some positive findings relating to localised, informal support that parenting courses or groups offer where mothers can ask the questions they may have. Again here, concerns were raised surrounding the perceived hidden agenda of professionals to promote aspects of parenting such as breastfeeding, meeting of developmental milestones and the connection this has to a developing feeling of pressure from participants. The need for neutral, empathetic and non-judgemental health professionals were consistently raised by participants.

Interpersonal surveillance was explored again within this theme in relation to the need for more honesty and removal of the '*rose tinted glasses*' (Ruth) between mothers about the challenges of modern motherhood. Issues were raised surrounding comparisons between mothers that are heightened through social media and celebrity culture. Awareness of the parenting industry but difficulty in resisting this (Henderson et al. 2015) was also demonstrated, this level of surveillance can be seen as, alongside structural surveillance, a contributing variable in the most powerful level of surveillance which was found within this research to be self-surveillance.

Theme 6 (the 'all-consuming' pressure to be 'super-mum') reinforced self-surveillance as the most powerful level of surveillance within modern motherhood with participants reporting a feeling of guilt and pressure to perform in a role that was perceived by society as natural, feel an instant connection and an '*overwhelming love*' (Clare). This self-surveillance developed into a worrying silence (Símonardóttir and Gíslason 2018) whereby for some participants, aspects of motherhood were deemed 'taboo' including annoyance at their child's challenging behaviour and finding the role difficult were not to be discussed. Opportunities were explored through returning to work, frustrations with partner and family members and concerns relating to post-natal depression all associated with the internalisation of society messages and the '*master narrative*' (Kerrick and Henry 2017, p. 1) of motherhood ideologies. A shift in confidence was noted as developing towards the end of the first year when participants reported feeling more relaxed, competent and demonstrated more awareness of the unhelpful implication of contradictory advice and wider parenting culture.

The final theme, theme 7 (reflection on motherhood) reinforced self-surveillance as the most powerful level of surveillance with fundamental aspects of resilience identified as being linked to the need for mothers to retain or regain their own sense of identity, develop their confidence through appropriate local support and resist the dominant discourse that motherhood is natural and instinctive for all women. Overall, internalisation of structural and interpersonal levels of surveillance (Henderson et al. 2010) resulted in the most powerful surveillance which is self-surveillance whereby, in Foucauldian terms, '*rights and obligations are established and imposed*' across members of society (Dreyfus and Rabinow 1982, p. 192). Within the exposure to the different levels of surveillance, there is a recognition that the reactions to these have a degree of autonomy within them that can be further nurtured through the building of confidence within this role. Rather than a prescriptive, one size fits all approach to motherhood, through support systems that encourage agency and individuality, mothers may be able to '*reflect upon the discursive relations which constitute her and the society in which she lives, and be able to choose from the options available*' (Weedon 1997, p. 121).

Future Research, Publications, Policy and Practice

It is important now to use this research, and any subsequent research, as a way of considering the support currently offered to mothers in the UK in relation to the implications of different forms of surveillance embedded within society on maternal well-being, identity and resilience. Through sharing the results of the research including the impact that social media has on the lives of new mothers, the essential role of an empathetic and neutral health professionals and early practitioners and the effect that the overwhelming influx of contradictory 'expert' advice has on sensitive aspects of motherhood including breastfeeding and the meeting of developmental milestone, it is possible to shine a light on these issues and bring a deeper awareness to those supporting new mothers. It is essential that those delivering parenting courses are able to be critically reflective and consider their practice and professionalism (Dyer 2016 in Czerniawski and Lofthouse 2018) in order to deliver the appropriate support for each mother they work with.

It is also important to provide opportunities for policy makers and practitioners to reflect on research and take proactive steps to avoid portraying motherhood at formulaic and homogenous at best, and as an ordeal at worst, with potentially disastrous implications if a mother somehow fails in her role. Instead, steps need to be taken towards supporting mothers to find the confidence in this role with appropriate, practical support, to feel 'good enough' (Winnicott 1964), retain their own identities and ultimately, enjoy the experience to its full potential. The overarching importance of proactive, neutral, practical support from health and early years professionals along with opportunities within the local area for mothers to share experiences and develop an honest, truthful, non-judgemental interpersonal support network are particularly important for new mothers.

Summary of Findings

The six key findings from this research are outlined below. With each key finding, provocations and recommendation are provided regarding the important next steps that must be taken in relation to the support currently offered to new mothers from early years practitioners, health professionals, policy and academia:

Key Finding 1: Parenting courses can provide opportunities for new mothers to build daily structure, social networks and reduce feelings of isolation.

Provocations and Recommendations: Localised support groups developed by qualified early years practitioners and health professionals are crucial. Such support groups must consider the views and experiences of new mothers, including a flexible approach to course delivery which responds to the diverse needs of group members.

Key Finding 2: Some negative experiences of parenting courses occur when practitioners are considered 'pushy' or 'non-neutral', particularly regarding sensitive areas such as breastfeeding or the reaching of developmental milestones. It is important that those professionals delivering universal parenting courses are well qualified, critically reflective practitioners that understand the needs of new mothers and young children and can deliver individualised support.

Provocations and Recommendations: Proactive, empathetic and practical support from health professionals and early years practitioners are needed. A move towards a graduate-led workforce of early years practitioners and health professionals that are encouraged, through policy, to recognise mothers and young children as individuals with differing needs, is essential.

Key Finding 3: Participants see a perceived place in society for parenting courses when they are practical, supportive, individualised and neutral rather than formulaic, homogenous or grounded in psychoanalytical or neurodevelopmental underpinnings, which can promote feelings of judgement or added pressure.

Provocations and Recommendations: The structure and underpinning theoretical base of parenting courses should be re-considered and centre around practical and flexible support developed in conjunction with well qualified early years practitioners, health professionals and new mothers, with recognition of the critical importance of the inclusion of the mothers' voice.

Key Finding 4: Findings link to the wider 'parenting culture' with societal pressures, motherhood ideologies, support or comparisons between mothers and other aspects of interpersonal surveillance e.g. social media, celebrity culture, adding to the challenge of finding confidence and agency within the role.

Provocations and Recommendations: Opportunities for further research include investigating the impact of social media on the mental health of mothers is vital and the findings of this research will be considered in relation to how it can be widely shared with new mothers, policy makers, academics, early years practitioners and health professionals.

Key Finding 5: Self-surveillance is identified as the most powerful aspect of modern motherhood. Challenges include, a reluctance to discuss 'taboo' aspects of motherhood such as challenges with instant attachment following birth, and the internalisation of social and cultural pressures.

Provocations and Recommendations: Any future universal parenting courses should include content which highlights the impact that structural, interpersonal and self-surveillance can have on new mothers. It is essential that this research is shared with new mothers as a way to shine a light and work towards reducing the damage that silences on taboo aspects of motherhood can have. This includes exploring opportunities to disseminate findings of this research to new mothers through health, early years education and social media channels.

Key Finding 6: It is important to note that, although there are clear levels of surveillance that are embedded into society, there was also evidence of agency and autonomy in the responses to these levels which were developed through strong social networks, support systems and the retaining of identity.

Provocations and Recommendations: Empowering opportunities are needed for new mothers to develop autonomy and confidence in an informal environment and foster trusting, interpersonal support networks. It is through these support systems that new mothers will continue to be able to recognise, resist and reshape the dominant discourses and ultimately, enjoy the experience to its full potential.

Reflections

This final section will consider the research process as a whole including what I, as a researcher have learnt through the application of the approach, methods and finally, reflections on the contribution to knowledge made from this research.

Feminist Post-structuralist Approach

Recognised as a potential *'contradiction in terms'* (Baxter 2003, p. 2), a feminist post-structuralist ontological and epistemological approach was taken within this research in order to allow the findings to be analysed with the potential for multiple possibilities to the reactions to different levels of surveillance (Henderson et al. 2010). This approach is described by Baxter (2003, p. 2) as a *'productive contribution'* which offers the opportunity for the experiences of women to be explored without the limitations of *'old assumptions'* (Baxter 2003, p. 2) as both philosophies share a *'common concern with subjectivity'* (Weedon 1997, p. 40). Within this perspective, the experiences of women in modern society can be explored in relation to the pressures from multiple perspectives specifically within this research, those pressures come from the different forms of surveillance that mothers are exposed to, i.e. structural, interpersonal and self-surveillance (Henderson et al. 2010) and how these pressures work within the different aspects of the panoptic machine (Foucault 1977) and serve to *'govern the soul'* (Rose 1999, p. 1).

Another advantage of analysing this research through a feminist post-structuralist perspective came from the possibility of exploring examples of resistance and agency within the reflections of mothers. The lack of recognition within the literature review of how women may use parenting education as a way to empower themselves, select the strategies that work from them and develop their own confidence proactively, were of concern. As reflected throughout this research, I felt that a purely Foucauldian or 'parenting culture' discourse (Furedi 2008; Lee et al. 2014) would do mothers a disservice. This was confirmed within the interviews with participants acknowledging that the parenting courses they attended were '*a lifeline*' (Gemma) for them at a time in which they needed this support. Over time, participants were eventually able to '*be a bit more decisive and thinking 'well, no that's not going to work for me... and this is why...*' (Louise). In these instances, rather than being '*hapless victims of actions wholly beyond their control*' (Nakano Glenn et al. 1994, p. 337), participants demonstrated that they reclaimed control and were '*capable of framing strategies to enhance their situation*' (Nakano Glenn et al. 1994, p. 337) Rather than being '*docile*' (Foucault 1977, p. 136), mothers were, within the constraints of a society that projects an ideology of motherhood as natural and instinctive, able to develop their own strategies and rebuild identities and confidence. Davis agrees that, within a feminist post-structuralist perspective it is possible to '*embrace the rich complexity of life lived through multiple and contradictory discourses*' (Davis 1997, p. 272) and agency is encouraged and promoted through the opportunity to share these experiences, give voice to and therefore disempower the '*silences on motherhood*' (O'Brien Hallstein 2008, p. 144).

As researcher I also learnt an important lesson during the early analysis stage. I have reflected upon my frustrations regarding the '*false start*' (Newby 2014, p. 473) that I experienced when, over the course of approximately 6 months, I tried to drive the data directly into the conceptual framework which resulted in a detachment to the individual responses of the participants. A more open interpretation was therefore applied during the second attempt which carefully identified issues that could later be categorised into themes. This was an important lesson for me as researcher and as I reflected on the importance of retaining the responses of participants at the heart of the study which in turn, complimented the feminist post-structuralist approach to the research.

Contribution to Knowledge

My ontological position, along with a methodology that centres around the experiences and voices of mothers makes this research an original contribution to knowledge. A review of the literature showed a gap in the research through the exploration of the dominant discourses, particularly in relation to listening to the experiences of new mothers through a more open, feminist post-structuralist worldview. Whilst there were many strong opinions and research surrounding the support that should be offered to new mothers, be it from the political promotion of parenting agenda, or through the contrasting suggestion that parenting agenda only serves to reinforce the message that parenting can be taught, there was limited research relating to asking new mothers to reflect on their experiences of attending a parenting course, leading to in-depth reflections on motherhood on a wider scale. By considering the experiences of modern motherhood from a feminist post-structuralist worldview and by keeping the voices of the mothers at the centre of this research, I was able to analyse both the constructs of modern motherhood and the varied responses to these experiences.

As a mother of children who were aged 2 and 3 when I began the professional doctorate I was able to identify with many of the responses from mothers during the interviews as I had been there myself fairly recently. I consider this experience to be an advantage within the research overall as it strengthened my ontological position and reinforced the relational elements of the interviews (Oakley 2005) that were fundamental to the feminist post-structuralist position within which this research was grounded. As stated by Ackerly and True (2008, p. 705) it is the responsibility of researchers to put '*our commitment to self-reflexivity, our attentiveness to the power of epistemologies, of boundaries and relationships into the practice of our research*'. From a feminist post-structuralist perspective, it is the development of a deeper understanding of the discursive practices that are so deeply embedded '*in particular society, at a particular moment, is the first step in intervening in order to initiate change*' (Weedon 1997, p. 131). Therefore, by exploring the experiences of mothers it has been possible to consider their experiences as socially constructed whilst also considering each woman as an agent of social change who can '*reflect upon the discursive relations which constitute her and the society in which she lives, and choose from the options available*' (Weedon 1997, p. 121).

The intention of the research remained throughout the lengthy process of the Doctor of Education programme and the completion of this book. The aim of exploring the experiences of mothers that have attended a universal parenting course and to provide a deeper insight into some of the social and cultural pressures that are embedded within modern motherhood. This research has provided this insight along with the potential for further research in relation to some of the individual issues and themes within the findings that need further exploration including the influence and impact of social media during the transition to motherhood, the impact of breastfeeding discourse and the fundamental role of health professionals and early years practitioners in supporting new mothers along with some of the challenges they face in finding their autonomy when they support new mothers. As I move forward to develop future research, the critical importance of hearing the reality of modern motherhood remains and this can only be done by continuing to provide opportunities for mothers to share their experiences and for those in positions of power to be encouraged to listen to these experiences in order to ensure that any support provided reflects the voices of those who really do know best, the mothers themselves.

References

Ackerly, B., & True, J. (2008). Reflexivity in Practice: Power and Ethics in Feminist Research on International Relations. *The International Studies Association, 10*(8), 693–707.

Baxter, J. (2003). *Positioning Gender in Discourse: A Feminist Methodology.* Hampshire: Palgrave Macmillan.

Beaupre Gillespie, B., & Schwartz Temple, H. (2011). *Good Enough Is the New Perfect.* Don Mills, ON, Canada: Harlequin.

Choi, P., Henshaw, C., Baker, S., & Tree, J. (2005). Supermum, Superwife, Supereverything: Performing Femininity in the Transition to Motherhood. *Journal of Reproductive and Infant Psychology, 23*(2), 167–180.

Clarke, B., Younas, F., & Project Team and Family Kids and Youth. (2017). *Helping Parents to Parent*. London: Social Mobility Commission.

Currie, J. (2008). Conditions Affecting Perceived Coping for New Mothers, Analysis of a Pilot Study, Sydney, Australia. *International Journal of Mental Health Promotion, 10*(3), 34–41.

Czerniawski, G., & Lofthouse, R. (Eds.). (2018). *Bera Bites Issue 1: Early Childhood*. London: British Education Research Association. Available at https://www.bera.ac.uk/publication/issue-1-early-childhood. Accessed 13 January 2020.

Davis, B. (1997). The Subject of Post-structuralism: A Reply to Alison Jones. *Gender and Education, 9*(3), 271–283.

Dreyfus, H. L., & Rabinow, P. (1982). *Michael Foucault: Beyond Structuralism and Hermeneutics*. London: Harvester Wheatsheaf.

Douglas, S. J., & Michaels, M. M. (2005). *The Mommy Myth: The Idealization of Motherhood and How It Has Undermined All Women*. New York: Free Press.

Foucault, M. (1977). *Discipline and Punish: The Birth of the Prison*. London: Penguin.

Furedi, F. (2008). *Paranoid Parenting: Why Ignoring the Experts May Be Best for Your Child*. Wiltshire: Continuum.

Henderson, A., Harmon, S., & Houser, J. (2010). A New State of Surveillance: Applying Michael Foucault to Modern Motherhood. *Surveillance and Society, 7*(3/4), 231–247.

Henderson, A., Harmon, S., & Newman, H. (2015). The Price Mothers Pay, Even When They Are Not Buying It: Mental Health Consequences of Idealized Motherhood. *Sex Roles, 74,* 512–526.

Johnson, R., & Wilson, H. (2012). Parents' Evaluation of 'Understanding Your Child's Behaviour', a Parenting Group Based on the Solihull Approach. *Community Practitioner, 85*(5), 29–33.

Kerrick, M., & Henry, R. L. (2017). 'Totally in Love': Evidence of a Master Narrative for How New Mothers Should Feel About Their Babies. *Sex Roles, 76*(1), 1–16.

Lee, E., Bristow, J., Faircloth, C., & Macvarish, J. (2014). *Parenting Culture Studies*. London: Palgrave Macmillan.

Nakano Glenn, E., Chang, G., & Rennie Forcey, L. (1994). *Mothering: Ideology, Experience and Agency*. New York: Routledge.

Newby, P. (2014). *Research Methods for Education* (2nd ed.). London: Routledge.

Oakley, A. (2005). *The Ann Oakley Reader*. Bristol: Policy Press.

O'Brien Hallstein, D. L. (2008). Silences and Choice: The Legacies of White Second Wave Feminist in the New Professoriate. *Women's Studies in Communication, 31*(2), 143–150.

Rose, N. (1999). *Governing the Soul: The Shaping of the Private Self* (2nd ed.). London: Free Association Books.

Símonardóttir, S., & Gíslason, I. V. (2018). When Breast Is Not Best: Opposing Discourses on Breastfeeding. *The Sociological Review, 66*(3), 1–7.

Weedon, C. (1997). *Feminist Practice and Poststructuralist Theory* (2nd ed.). Oxford: Blackwell Publishers.

Winnicott, D. (1964). *The Child, the Family and the Outside World*. London: Penguin Books.

Correction to: Surveillance of Modern Motherhood

Correction to:
H. Simmons, *Surveillance of Modern Motherhood*,
https://doi.org/10.1007/978-3-030-45363-3

The original version of the book was inadvertently published with incorrect abstracts, which have now been corrected.

The updated version of the book can be found at https://doi.org/10.1007/978-3-030-45363-3

C1

Index

A

Advice 2, 4, 5, 14, 15, 33–40, 42, 43, 45, 48–55, 60–63, 67, 74, 76, 77, 80, 81, 84–86, 94, 95, 97–103, 105, 115, 121–123, 126, 131, 137, 149, 150, 154, 159, 160, 162, 163

Attachment 35, 38, 68, 71, 95, 96, 126, 130, 132, 165

B

Baby manuals 2, 4, 33, 38, 49, 63, 95, 123, 160

Bonding 126, 146

Breastfeeding 43, 45, 46, 50, 53, 83–87, 93, 97, 100, 102, 103, 105–109, 123, 131, 145–147, 149, 150, 160, 161, 163, 164, 169

C

Celebrity culture 100, 112, 115, 161, 165

Children's Centre 7, 8, 48, 51, 64, 66, 75, 149, 151

Comparisons 82, 83, 85, 124, 150, 161, 165

Confidence 43, 44, 48, 54, 55, 82, 88, 89, 103, 108, 123, 126, 133, 137, 138, 146, 148, 160–163, 165, 167

Culture 4, 25, 49, 71, 93, 98, 107, 115, 138

D

Disciplinary technologies 20, 135

Dominant discourse 2, 4, 10, 15, 19, 20, 25–28, 30, 55, 73,

103, 106, 115, 123, 131, 135,
152, 154, 160, 162, 166, 168

E

Early years 15, 61, 81, 104, 107,
108, 160, 163–165, 169
Empowerment 29, 78, 100, 122,
136, 160
Expert 1, 4, 9, 20, 33–35, 37–39,
42, 45, 54, 55, 63, 94, 97, 98,
103, 115, 123, 126, 138, 154,
159, 163

F

Feminism 26–28, 121, 160
Feminist post-structuralism 19, 29

G

Good enough mother 89, 102, 120,
125
Government 2, 5, 9, 21, 59, 60,
62–65, 69, 74, 78, 79, 90, 93,
94, 97, 99, 154, 160

H

Health professionals 14, 50, 53, 62,
70, 81, 93, 100–107, 138,
149, 151, 160, 161, 163–165,
169
Health visitor 14, 38, 48, 50–53, 61,
105, 124, 149, 150
Hierarchy 108, 111

I

Identity 11, 12, 27, 112, 132, 133,
137, 138, 148, 151, 162, 163,
165
Ideologies 20, 25, 37, 38, 41, 42,
54, 85, 96, 110, 115, 116,
124, 128, 130, 131, 135, 159,
162, 165, 167
Industry 53, 95, 100, 114, 115, 123,
161
Instinct 34, 36, 37, 54, 55, 86, 98,
126, 137
Interpersonal 26, 40, 82–84, 100,
108, 111, 112, 115, 119,
124–126, 136, 152, 161–163,
165, 166
Intrapersonal 119

J

Judgement 20–24, 26, 27, 42, 54,
63, 84, 85, 87, 101, 106, 108,
109, 119, 124–126, 128, 161,
164

M

Master narrative 26, 28, 107, 152,
162
Media 5, 22, 93, 95, 97, 98, 100,
113–115, 122
Midwife 52
Motherhood 1–7, 10, 11, 15, 19,
20, 22, 23, 25–30, 33, 34,
36–38, 41–45, 47–49, 52, 55,
64, 65, 71, 73, 77, 78, 93, 96,
97, 100–102, 106, 109–113,
115, 116, 119–121, 123–126,
128, 130, 131, 133, 135–138,

143–149, 152–154, 159–163,
    165, 167–169

N
Neuroscience 71–73, 79, 96
Normalisation 28, 38, 59, 74, 94,
    112

O
Observation 21, 22, 87, 136
Oppression 29, 78

P
Panoptism 20
Parenting 1, 2, 4–6, 9, 10, 15,
    21–25, 27, 28, 33–40, 48,
    51–53, 55, 59–89, 93–111,
    114–116, 120–124, 126,
    130–132, 134–136, 148, 151,
    152, 160, 161, 163, 164, 167,
    168
Parenting culture 4, 10, 29, 53, 71,
    77, 78, 93, 96, 98–100, 120,
    162, 165, 167
Photo elicitation interviews 5, 6, 93,
    119, 143
Political intervention 60, 65, 74, 90
Post-natal depression 126, 134, 135,
    146, 147, 162
Post-structuralism 19, 20, 28, 160
Power 2, 7, 11, 12, 20, 21, 24,
    28–30, 63, 70, 71, 79, 94,
    105, 106, 115, 124, 128, 135,
    169

Pressure 2, 15, 22, 23, 34, 38, 41,
    43, 45–48, 53, 60, 85, 94–96,
    100, 101, 104, 106–110,
    112–116, 119, 121, 124–133,
    135, 143, 144, 147–150, 154,
    161, 164–166, 169
Problematisation 34, 64
Professionalisation 2, 34, 64, 107,
    122

S
Silences 131, 138, 165
Social class 64
Social media 4, 33, 39–42, 100,
    101, 110–113, 115, 122, 154,
    161, 163, 165, 169
State 6, 22, 40, 52, 72, 78, 94, 95,
    100
Support 5, 6, 10, 14, 15, 20, 34, 38,
    40, 42, 47–53, 59–65, 68–70,
    74, 78, 81, 85, 94, 97, 98,
    102, 103, 105, 107, 120, 122,
    149, 151, 154, 161, 163–165
Surveillance 2–5, 15, 20–23, 26, 27,
    29, 33, 39, 40, 45, 63, 72,
    78, 82–84, 94, 97, 100, 105,
    108, 109, 111–113, 116, 119,
    124–126, 133, 135–138, 148,
    152–154, 161–163, 165, 166

T
Taboo 126, 129–131, 162, 165
Transition 34, 43, 47, 113, 120,
    137, 143, 169

U

Universal parenting course 2, 3, 5, 7, 8, 15, 43, 66, 67, 69, 73, 78, 90, 123, 164, 165, 169

V

Value 61, 63, 76, 93, 96, 97, 100, 124

Voice 10, 99, 152, 165, 167–169

CPI Antony Rowe
Eastbourne, UK
August 26, 2020